CW00923719

Published by Veronica Anja Shaw

113 Mill Bridge Close, Retford, DN22 6FE

This is a First Edition of 100 copies.

For a copy please contact me on, vswritingthoughts@yahoo.com

ISBN 978-1-913319-33-5

Printed by Book Empire
www.bookempire.co.uk
Unit 7, Lotherton Way, Garforth, Leeds, LS25 2JY

Printed in Great Britain

Foreword.

Yesterday I went to Boots and very cheekily asked one of the lovely ladies working there to break the quarantine rules for Corona V. "Could I please be cheeky and ask for a bar of Chanel No 5 soap?" "I know it's naughty, but I really need something to make me feel girlie and normal".

The lady obliged, with a smile saying, "as long as customers knows what they want we are happy to help." God love her. I just wanted to feel clean and special again. Amazing how something so simple could bring me so much of a lift.

The last past few months of writing this has taken an enormous amount of energy and pain. I have had to dig really deep. Re calibrate myself several times and remind myself why I set out to write this when the Dark days visited me.

To begin my recovery from anxiety and depression and enable others to have hope, I realised I needed to do something different. In the absence of any current professional help, I thought I would try and achieve the discovery of the past traumas in my life which have shaped my personality. It has been incredibly painful. I don't like some of the things I've found out about myself and the past which I have subconsciously spent years pushing to the back of my troubled brain

It has been much like many of my adventures and lessons in life. I have learnt from many others along the way, valuable lesson to achieve the survival game. To succeed in life and move on, I know I have to do this to come out the other side. I do not know what the other side looks like yet, but every adventure has its rewards.

Twelve years ago, I was persuaded, over a much needed double vodka and tonic, in the Eagle bar in London after work, to climb to base camp of Everest for a "Breakfast at Base Camp" for a soon to be special friends' charity. My friend said, "come on it will be a Hoot!". Oh, it was that, and much much… more.

It was a light bulb moment that changed my outlook on my life. Climbing Everest with all its natural beauty, was not like any other mountain I had climbed. It was hard, a massive endurance test, challenging painful and tearful at times.

Like many adventures in my life it was a journey I needed to achieve. To be who I am today. Failure was not an option.

Who said Survival is easy? It certainly is not.

To everyone throughout my life up until now and those yet to help me further shape it, I want to thank you all for the strength and values you have reinforced in my life. Every precious adventure we have shared together, from my brothers to my amazing son and his wonderful family. My friends, colleagues and every human being who has touched my life and shared the journey with me for enabling me to complete this novel.

To my amazing mother, Helena Kowalczk Nesteruk who was taken from us far too young and I was never able to share my growing years with, I dedicate this book.

Without her strength and survival instincts, strong independent, adventurous spirit, and family values I would never have been able to have continued my life's adventures. I know you are up there somewhere mum, wagging your arthritic finger at me sometimes and sometimes smiling with such pride at me. I am so grateful to have had you as my role model.

I often wonder if you wore the Dark Hat and how you managed to keep pushing it off.

Love you always,

your Anja XXX

Chapter 1

The Dark Hat

Traditionally a hat is worn to suit a person's unique personality. Of which I have many which I wear with different moods. The Dark Hat is different, it denotes my degree of depression. It comes and goes at its own discretion. Sometimes if hovers in the distance as a reminder of what's to come. It does not do to ignore the Dark Hat. When it visits, we should all beware!

9th October 2019 9.15 am

Chesterfield

Sitting alone like Billy no mates, in my garden chair, staring at my beautiful garden, my bottom sinks ever deeper into my seat as do my brain cells sinking, ever deeper into their own particular brand of mush and confusion. The beauty of the flowers is lost on me today.

Memories come flooding back, of a gas mask and a dentist holding it closely against a twelve-year old panicking face, my face, to anesthetize me to aid in the extraction of a few teeth.

The terribly strange sinking feeling of being swallowed up by a cavernous cyclone in my throat, being dragged to its very epicentre the strange dizziness invades my head and suddenly I disappear into the abyss. My thoughts are dark very dark.

The Dark Hat is pulled fully over my head and ears. Hugging me for dear life to keep me safe. It won't move. It feels like it's superglued in place.

After a peaceful few day staying with Kurt (My current boyfriend of five months) at his flat in Retford, sitting in the sunshine talking and drinking beer outside a pub in the remainder of the autumn sunshine I felt almost normal. The Dark Hat does not visit so much while I am with him.

Yet coming back home to Chesterfield today the sinking feeling returns like a big bass drum. My brain can't see the beauty of the pink hydrangea bush, which covers the white double garage doors in front of me. Nurtured, by my excessive watering, due to the unusually dry spring and summer this year.

To achieve this beauty, I had to continuously water it to stop it drying up all the time. It was such a thirsty plant. The only way I could quench its

2

thirst was to put the water hose end in the plant pot and leave it there every evening for at least five minutes until it was soaked through. (It had outgrown its pot due to the amazing Miracle Grow I've been feeding it.)

I am so proud to say it worked. The, bush was nearly the size of the white double doors. A miracle indeed! Too heavy to move it has to stay there.

Yet even with something so beautiful in front of me, The Dark Hat which started on top of my head and has quickly travelled down to cover my eyes and is pulling ever tighter over my head. I'm staring at the beautiful flowers but don't see them or their true beauty. The hanging deep red geranium baskets at either side of the bush still surviving the cooler autumn weather completes a picture of a beautiful creation. My stuck brain only returns to dark thoughts, the past….and the fear of loneliness and how the hell do I get rid of this Dark Hat?

The Dark Hat is rigidly fixed to my head now, it will not move. Its superglue effect is tighter bringing with it the worrying tingling in my right back brain.

I sit in my relaxing garden chair and try to enjoy the last of the sunny weather with my coffee and cigarette. I wonder if it is my return to Chesterfield after twenty years absence that has triggered all these dark reactions? Or is it the enormity of the gardening work I want to do but cannot.

My friend Anna thinks it's the rejection of so many job applications and the enormous effort I have put into them. She could be right. I have never questioned it before.

I sit rigid in my chair the jobs piling up in my brain, my body not moving. Time goes on around me, the ashtray gets fuller, yet I still sit here trying to urge my body to make some sense of which action I should take next. There will be no movement. I sit here for hours still and in another world. The Dark Hat has completely consumed me now. How long have I sat there; I really don't know?

Chapter 2

Broken... a trigger or one of the many?

June 2012 10.00 am

Bridge Cottage, Ainsworth

Five minutes before I have to jump in my car to go to work at the Co-op. My retirement job I really love. I noticed that I have just enough time to water a very dry plant I must have missed during last night's mammoth watering session. The garden was more than thirsty. It was gaging, drawing the water in faster than I could cover it.

I grab the aluminium ladder outside my kitchen window and bang it against the stone pillar where the plant is. Imbedded over six food high in the stone pillar, I built to enable it to cascade. down from. I race up the ladder with my watering jug in my hand without thinking to check it was secure. The ladder started to slip a little. I should have stopped right then to check its stability but in my haste to get to work on time, I just continued. I really didn't think I was that high up that I could do any real damage.

I stretch my arm to try and reach the newly planted Campanula blue star shaped flowers, from the Dalmatian Mountains in Croatia. They are my favourite. I am so eager to get them embedded I could not wait to see the image of their beauty cascading down the stone post. So, consumed by this my sense of health and safety went out of the window, only the vision of the purply blue view from my kitchen window drove me to continue. I visualised them trailing down the six-foot stone pillar, a cascade of beauty. I was lost in their impending beauty and determined the post I had built especially for them would fulfil its true potential and my vision.

In my haste in trying to achieve this I must have incorrectly placed the ladder against the wall. Every time I stretched to water a bit more of the pillar the ladders edged a little further away from the wall. Gently scrapping against the stone post. I wanted to soak the new flowers. Today, was going to be warm. I needed to prevent them from dying of thirst while I was out at work on this beautiful summer's day. It was a simple task. It was a labour of love I would live to regret and still am.

While lost in my imagination of how amazing the stone pillar would look with the beautiful purply blue, little star flowers starting to appear day by day…. I hear a creak………then another creak the ladder moved with speed towards the floor with me on it. Hindered by a stone urn, below me, which broke my fall, in the worst possible way.

The pains shooting up my ankle were excruciating. Tangled up in the ladder half in a large stone urn and half in the plant with soil everywhere I am well and truly stuck. Fuck I can't move the pain is the worst hell I've ever felt. This is real pain. The minute I try to move my foot it just gets worse. Pains just shoot everywhere around my ankle. I am in shear agony. Tears of pain are streaming down my face.

I felt like a million daggers were stabbing into my foot from different directions every conceivable part of me is screaming at me with every slight movement. I know I need to drag myself somehow out of this mess. I keep telling my brain to move my body. It stubbornly refuses. I think the pain is leading that decision! I lay there paralyzed, frightened to move.

I am well and truly stuffed. No phone on me, no one else in the house. I am in a part of the garden which couldn't be seen from the road. No one could hear me shouting from the golf course across the river. Even if someone does hear my pathetic cries, they wouldn't be able to see me through the overgrown bushes on the riverbank.

It took me over thirty minutes to gradually drag myself up the conservatory steps to get indoors the tears were relentless. I dragged myself a distance of over twenty feet including dragging my foot up two wide steps. The air was blue! Each, movement was hell on earth.

Inch by inch shooting pain tears of agony with every move makes my progress slow.

I finally reached the kitchen exhausted and sweating. Beside myself with pain, I managed to raise myself enough to grab a tea cloth to draw my mobile phone nearer by whacking it several times to get it closer and eventually onto the floor. Finally, it comes to the edge of the kitchen cupboard and I drag it off and catch it, to dial 999. I then collapsed in a heap on the kitchen floor. I am completely exhausted.

The Police asked so many questions. I just wanted them to send an ambulance and give me an injection of something, anything to stop the pain.

The other problem I forgot to mention was the front door was locked and they would not be able to get in.

Luckily, Gillian, my friend from across the road at the pub has a spare key. I rang her and asked her to look out for the ambulance and let them in.

The memories of the stupidity of the fall and the impact it left on my future life have lived with me ever since. So many life changing decisions had to be made. Just for the sake of a plant and a beautiful view from my kitchen window. No more heels, no more mountain.

Both the journey to the hospital and the Bolton Accident and Emergency (A&E) experience were a nightmare along with the past eight years of living with arthritis in the joint and no real help to enable me to change my career which I'd only really just begun at the Co-operative.

It had been my intention when I took my early retirement at fifty years old to take a less stressful job and one where I could be a gentler, kinder customer facing person. I wanted to help little old ladies and gents, across the road with their shopping. Spend the time with them, that they dearly deserved. Help them to get a great customer experience while visiting my one day own managed shop.

Gardening, walking, building, climbing, and going to the gym were my de stresses. I love to do all of them as a form of relaxation. I built beautiful stonework inside and out of my last cottage. Everyday light minute when I got home in summer was spent creating more features inside and out. My garden was always praised for its beauty and hard work.

My ability to be on my feet for long since my stupid accident is minimal. As is my leg flexibility to bend at the ankle joint. The pain is continually excruciating. I have been through Physiotherapy, warm swimming pool exercising, shoe inserts, going to the gym to keep it moving and steroid and pain killer injections. The latter was the only success to lift the pain. It was like being in seventh heaven for about three months. No pain whatsoever. Absolute bloody heaven! I used to wake up in the morning thinking NO Pain! Yes!! Do something quick while you can before the pain comes backs.

Unfortunately, the Consultant at Bolton General who was dealing with me wasn't happy to keep giving the injections to me. (I've only had three in eight years) He felt It wouldn't be good for my foot when it eventually would need a fusion operation. Which I will not even consider. Given that I would be totally disabled, have to walk with a stick, not be able to drive at all and even more vulnerable.

Up to a few months ago I was still driving. Given it was getting harder and more painful with every journey, it still helped me with shopping and trying to find a job. My main problem was that my foot would decide to freeze while I was driving, which can be a bit inconvenient when in traffic. I had to take the decision that I needed to stop for everyone's safety. Sadly, I sold my car and with it my independence.

Learning to travel on the train and bus again unfortunately heightened my anxiety. Hence my adventures out became less frequent. I felt too vulnerable. Too close to people. I didn't want to speak to them or hear their conversations. I just lost the plot. It was difficult enough trying to get to train stations and allow time for my slow plodding to get to the platforms on time, but it was just the people. I couldn't cope with them seeing me being such a Slow Slug (SS).

People don't show any understanding for someone in a railway station who is confused and struggling to get around railway stations. They just pushed and shoved you. I'd had enough. It wasn't the world I wanted to be in. I would start sweating and having full blown anxieties that someone was going to rob me as I struggled. I would always be hatching a plan in my brain as to which bag, I would hit them with if they tried to steal my precious computer which went everywhere with me.

I really was hyper all the time. The pain was relentless, I would jerk my foot or stop, and my brains was making life even worse. It really was hopeless. I gave up. There was no one more pleased than me when Corona V isolation started.

Having tried to get help for this current disability over the years with Personal Independence Payment from the government (PIP) and now, I know that there will be no help with getting my true mobility back. I often wonder how others have managed to get cars and help but know that the system has totally exhausted me physically and mentally with the application process. The face to face meeting with their doctor has had me in tears. The questions were so evasive, and I was feeling so low having to explain everything.

The lady who performed the assessment said that maybe they could help with some adjustments to a vehicle. But this same lady, totally miss wrote my report. Either that or sent someone else's in. I was staggered when I got a copy to read.

I did originally want the assessment recording but decided to have faith in the system. What a Wally I am!! It's a good job I took Cheryl (Che's Scout leader and a friend of too many years to remember) with me as a witness.

Otherwise I do not think they would have believed me when I challenged their original assessment results. None, of the report bore a resemblance to the anxiety I went through for over an hour. Or the many tears of emotion it brought me.

The allowance they gave me was so small it would never be enough for me to get a vehicle I could drive now, never mind one with special adjustments. It barely pays for taxis to doctors, shopping and for medications. Never mind, someone to help in the garden and the house with hoovering and ironing. Not that I'd want anyone in my house. I wasn't ready to cope with that. I didn't really want to apply for it.

The whole process was advised by doctor with the help of the Citizens Advice (CA). Telling me I shouldn't be worrying about finances they would get me help as I should and am entitled to it and needed help financially at this time to help me recover from my trauma. I just wanted to be well and get back to finding a job. But the doctor insisted that until I rest it would not happen and my brain was telling me that.

I did challenge my initial assessment and got a slightly better deal, but it still wasn't what I had been advised I was entitled to. It won't give me the quality of life I need and get me back to work. I really don't think anything will now. My anxiety is just too high at the moment. I feel as if I am the only person no one wants to help. Treatment for my trauma is expensive and long. If only someone had spotted it sooner. It's something I should have had years ago.

So, I write and pray someone will get strength from my experience and get help when advised and its available to them.

Given how much tax and National insurance I have paid over the years. It really saddens me that we live in a world where some of us contribute so much to the economy over the years and when we really need help there is none to be had. It has already gone to others, so sad.

While now both my legs get worse daily because I have had to push one to support the other over the years of pain and my back is absolutely taking the piss when I want to stand for long. I have to 'suck it up' as some would say. Unless I agree to have fusion, I am stuffed.

So here I am sucking it up. I must get my act together, I know that. I wish my bloody brain would suck it up and bloody well engage and stop all these crappie negative thoughts. Why is it deciding to torment me, now when there is all this beauty in front of me? All this beauty is my work, why can I not take some pleasure from it. The Bloody Dark Hat! That is why.

All the pots and buckets filled with colourful plants are all my own handy work from days when I could do a little more. All the containers were found in the garage and around the garden. Sadly deserted, by its past deceased owner. I have brought them all back to life, having achieved all this when I first arrived here. Before the Dark days began.

Then my life was full of positivity and enthusiasm. At first, I wasn't sure if moving back to Chesterfield was the right decision, but I was really pleased with my decision and to be near my

13

friends. Full of positivity that I would get a job to subsidise my small pension and enjoy the garden and living next to farms, hearing the Cockerel crow in the morning and the peacocks at night. Be near the flat fields after struggling in a first floor flat with the stairs for a full year. Carrying the shopping upstairs with no lift was always a challenge and detrimental to my ankle arthritis.

This house I am in now is perfect. Full, of previous love and attention. Hand built by a friend's granddad; it was an honour to live here. Its many nooks and crannies, both inside and out, made it ideal for all my furniture which had been in storage for over a year. It was good to have my things around me at last.

Lots of outside space, for me to sit and enjoy the fresh air. A place to turn into a vegetable patch. The downstairs toilet really put the icing on the cake. I was by now really struggling with stairs and the sudden need to go to the loo.

Toilets can be special places when age and whoops moments take over. I was so looking forward to spending my next seven working years here until I had enough money to go to Spain and retire in the White Mountains. My dream. The plan was perfect, I would be able to write in the fresh air and enjoy the wonderful village life. I really wanted my grandchildren to have a place they could come and visit me and enjoy wonderful six-week holidays to enjoy its beauty and peace. It had always been my dream. To be part of the White Village family of people in Spanish White Villages and be there with my children. The beauty and welcoming of the people there are second to none. Not to mention the food and wine. A truly relating experience. Something everyone should experience at least once in their lifetime.

Chapter 3

Suck it up!

Start living with my illness and others!

13th October 2019 10.16 am Retford Kurt's

Today I woke up with a headache and an angry head. All my anger directed at Kurt and his violent television viewing (men's films). I feel like I'm being obsessed with the need to be loved by him. He is so kind and patient with me. I feel like I am an unreasonable controlling infection who wants to take over. So, selfish and unreasonable. I'm trying to keep my mouth shut. I feel I'm hurting him. For the first time in 3 months, we're so close what is up with me?

I knew this day would come when my illness would try to ruin things. I must get a grip.

I just want to make love to him all the time and make him feel good. Every time I look at him, he makes me tingle. I want to touch him and cuddle. It's obviously not his priority. Kurt is simply happy to have me here with him looking after me. He likes me just the way I am. That is a beautiful thing to say to someone. Especially feeling the way I do.

My crazy brain goes into overdrive. Seriously … what is wrong with me. Just writing this my arms start to get pins and needles. Maybe he just wants to chill, or his kneecap injury is causing him pain. I really worry myself with my thoughts.

I am normally so easy going and chilled about relationships. Why am I being so unreasonable this time? Don't I know a good person when I meet them? Obviously not!

Is the psychologist, I am seeing right? Are all my past memories coming back to haunt me? Will I ever be able to hold down a normal relationship? It is not looking that way. Haunting memories make me behave so unreasonably.

Dreams that seem to keep reoccurring since my visit to the psychologist were always the bad ones. The failed relationships. The bad boy relationships which should have been so out of character but were not. I was a total rebel. My need to escape home in teenage years drove me to do the strangest things in the name of love.

I am slowly beginning to understand why and feeling a little sick at the hurt I would have caused my mother.

Chapter 4

The Great Escape
Broke my Mothers heart.
August 1977
Birmingham

My third boyfriend (Yes, I went through them like a dose of salts, even at the age of sixteen) and the one I gave everything to was both a liar and an abuser and to top it all broke my mother's heart. A married man with an adopted child? What was I thinking? Seriously!

Truthfully, I did not know he was married until I had fallen hook line and sinker.

I was born of Polish and German immigrants who had both survived the war in their own way and had both had their own personal Great Escape in 1944 although little was allowed to be discussed about it at home.

My mother, Helena Kowalczyk was a teacher in Germany and climbed over the Tatra Mountains in Zakopane to escape Hitler during the war and the communist Russians. My father, Piotr Nesteruk was in the army from being fifteen years old. He joined just after his whole family died of some plague at such a young age. He lied about his age so he could join up. Or so he said. Things were never as they seemed with father. Cobwebs keep coming out of the cupboard cup board since his death.

War was not a subject my father would allow us to talk about at home. Life at home was like being in the army. My father ruled with an iron fist or whatever he could pick up when the mood took him. I suppose he did not know any other way. Being in the army all those years it was the only life he knew.

My two brothers Peter and Andrew and myself were beaten regularly if we did not do as we were told. A black well-worn leather strap and buckle was our pain inflictor. I remember it well. One of the few things I can remember from my childhood.

My mother was not immune from his cruelty either if she didn't do as she was told he would beat her too. While, my eldest brother and I were still at home, we would shout from the top of the upstairs banister while cowering behind it with our fingers crossed. Just to make him aware that we could hear his threats. It didn't make any difference, he would then threaten us, and mother would be upset.

I swore to myself many a time that if I ever had children and a man behaved like that, I would leave him. I didn't want any child of mine to live through that sort of anxiety and fear that we did throughout our childhood. Hiding on the stairs instead of being in bed sleeping. Anxiously, listening to make sure everything was fine before we could go to sleep. To make sure there was no arguing. It was hell on earth. For every one of us, like living on pins.

My Mother and father were as different as chalk and cheese. Mum was a lady, well educated, cultured, and refined, elegantly dressed and father was a farm labourer a brute. He typically wanted to give an appearance that he was the educated one. But sadly, he was not. The façade never upheld itself. After thirty years of living in the UK his English was still not so good.

Father was a typical Gemini. One minute he was the nicest person in the world, kind and loving. Beautifully dressed, elegant, then whether it was from alcohol or some poison in his system from his shrapnel wounds (I really don't know) he would flare up for no reason at all.

His rages were always violent. Poor Mum was usually the brunt of his anger. She was always trying to protect her precious children. It must have been like walking from one war torn country into another with my father.

My father was the only man my mother had ever had a relationship with. Getting married at forty-one, I really think came as a real shock to her. As a teacher she always wanted children. My fathers' interest was more in making them and sometimes with force. Hence, all three of us were born in quick succession.

After my youngest brother was born, we all went into foster homes as Mother had to have a breast removed and the major operation due to cancer. Which in those days was a sheer act of terrorism to a woman's body? I remember her showing me the scar when I was thirteen and she was still devastated about how it looked and the pads and special bras she had to wear. It broke her heart.

Her life was not a happy one. With a husband who was jealous of her love for her Children and constantly flew into jealous rages her life was not just a cancer battle but a battle ground at home. None of us ever knew what we would walk into when we came home from school.

Needless to say, we had all left home by the time we were sixteen. (Mums life, requires a lot more research and my mother's German diary translating for another time when I am less sensitive)

My third boyfriend, I'll call him (B3X) was the most gorgeous man at the local dance I managed to escape too on a Saturday night. With my ten shillings I had earned, after a day of cleaning the house, ironing for five of us and baking for the week I needed to escape. I managed to persuade my mother to let me go to a dance and my father although not best pleased he didn't want to be the one to say no.

I had seen the dance advertised in a pub near a friend's house and initially went with her. Then when she could not come with me, I started going on my own just to escape home and have something to look forward to.

Now when I think about it, I must have been desperate to get away, to walk all that way, fifteen minutes to the bus and then a ten minute bus ride to get there. I paid my one shilling to get in and then stood at the bar on my own. A very brave thing to do, given I was only sixteen. I shouldn't have legally been there. It was dark and I mingled in. I meet a few guys while going there.

Unfortunately, or not, B3X was the one. I flirted with him outrageously. I was looking for someone to love me. I wanted B3X and meant to have him. Older than me by eight years (Always my attracted species over the years)It was almost as if I was looking for love from an older man. At the time I didn't understand why.

I wanted him so passionately and there was just no stopping me. So much so that I persuaded him to sneak into my house and be my first lover while my parents were out.

All sense of propriety and decency went out of the window with him. My parents would have killed me if they had ever found out. I don't know to this day how I did it. Maybe I wanted to get caught? Who knows how far my madness goes? The journey of discovery continues!

It wasn't the most mind-blowing experience the Mills & Boon stories had predicted. I think I thought I'd achieved a sense of rebellion. But total satisfaction wasn't achieved. I did however believe that this man loved me and was honoured as I'd given him something precious.

The months that followed were filled with running away from home, violence, hard work on my part working in a fish and chip shop. Going home on a bus every night and stinking of grease.

Not really the fairy tale life of passion and love I'd had expected. Pain hardship and pure survival instinct kept me going and the inability to admit I had made a massive mistake. Putting up with his violent behaviour, bulling, and many threats towards me, I had to admit now, that I was scared of him. But driven with the knowledge that I could fix this I carried on taking this and making excuses for his lies and deceit.

This man who had weed on me during the night when he had had too much to drink was not a suitable match. To top it all when I woke him up one night, he had the audacity to blamed me for it and started to bully and become violent again. By this time, his attractiveness had disappeared. I think the smell did that.

Today I still cannot believe what I did to be with him. Who can ever understand a young person's brain? When I think of my behaviour my poor mother must have been so ashamed when B3X's wife came to see her at our family home. To disclose that, I had broken up her marriage after I ran away with her husband to Chesterfield.

I was beyond wild and so eager to escape the arguments at home and violence I walked straight into a relationship that was just as bad.

Chapter 5

How to escape one monster?
Find a much worse one!
Che – With New Life come new hopes!

July 1979 – Chesterfield

Che, my only son (Read on you will find out later) was just three months old. He was born on the 16th May 1979 at 8.15am at Ashgate Nursing Hospital.

After an hour and a half of what I thought was constipation during the night. Even though, I was nearly four weeks overdue. (Yes, I know, der... not having any previous baby experience and where was this water breaking business? Anyway...No sign) I decided to ring the hospital. They sent an ambulance straight away.

The pain was not that bad I did not think. Given all the horror stories I had heard and my history of a nervous stomach and constipation from the iron tablets. I really didn't think the baby was coming.

At 6.30am. The poor ambulance crew thought I would have my child in the ambulance. Ken (Che's father) had just returned from work wet through. He asked me if he should come with me and I told him to get a bath, warm up and get some sleep, the

24

baby would be ages yet. (Or so I thought) Experience has a lot to answer for.

The ambulance men had a vastly different idea. They were panicking that I would have the baby in the ambulance. Oh dear. That's a really big Whoops! Maybe I should have gone to more baby classes?

Well I didn't disgrace myself by having the baby in the ambulance due to ignorance on my part, but I would have done had my delivery channel been big enough. Lucky ambulance men!

Once in the Ashgate nursing home, after much pushing and screaming, no baby, the gas didn't help either. (Maybe because we found out after the baby was born that it was empty) There was much talk about sending me to Scarsdale hospital. I don't think so. I told them that my doctor and I had discussed that if there were any complications, he would be happy to come to Ashgate Nursing home and deliver the child.

So, I tested him at his word. The midwives phoned my then doctor and he came straight away. While we were waiting for the doctor, I had to try to stop pushing. Kind of difficult, when the baby was eager to join us in the world to suddenly put the brakes on!

Once the doctor arrived pleasantries aside, he said I needed to be cut open to get the baby out as he was too big to get. Poor little thing! So, after some needles to numb the areas we finally got there. One healthy horrible mess! Urgh. I told them to take him away and wash him. Ok so I didn't know that babies came out all mucky. I really was a not very well informed about babies. I think, now I know I pissed off the midwives.

After being stitched up again, I was put in a private room upstairs next to the delivery room. The doctor came to see me, and I thanked him. I did ask to see my baby, but he said I should rest, I'd had a bad birth and the midwives would bring him up later. Ok, so I got out a packet of cigarettes and had a much needed cigarette after that horrendous screaming experience. I had a packet in my hospital bag that I'd been saving for the whole nearly ten months. The room from the view was lovely, open fields and the sun was shining. I opened the window and breathed in the lovely freshly cut grass.

My new baby still hadn't been brought up to see me and it was visiting time. When Ken came into the room, he said he had seen him, and he was gorgeous. I saw red. I wanted to see him. I asked one of the Nurses who showed Ken upstairs if I could have my baby brought up. She offered to bring us all coffee or tea. I didn't want bloody tea. I wanted to see my bloody baby. I'm afraid I slightly lost it. I did raise my voice.

When he wasn't brought up by the end of visiting, I got down the stairs with Kens help, sore with stiches and the aesthetic wearing off and I went to the nursery. There he was baby Che Kelly. Someone had named him. I asked who? They said his father. Oh, Nice to be consulted.

He was absolutely beautiful. Not the traumatised mucky little thing I saw earlier. He started to cry. I shouted the nurse. Shit I needed to learn how to do this. She told me to pick him up. I was scared of hurting him. Luckily, the nurse came and wrapped him up in a blanket and brought him out of his plastic box and put him in my arms. That was it. I was hooked instantly.

Ken & I have had many ups and downs until this point. The smile on my baby's face and his contentment gave me the courage and hope that his father would grow to share this love I have for him. The accident, Ken made me keep by threatening to hate me if I got rid of him at the young age of nineteen, having just lost my mother was going to be the happiest child I could make him.

That's the day Ken's control began. I had just walked away from a relationship with a good-looking Irishman who hit me and pissed on me in bed after a drinking session. Now I had jumped into another form of abuse with ZZ Top look alike. Great!! A bloody jealous obsessed; control freak was my son's dad. Only I could do this. This was the start of many disastrous, disjointed journeys of love I fell into.

Chapter 6

My retirement moves!

March 31st 2019– Lancaster

My last few trips up and down the tormenting stairs from my flat to the car were a killer. Gladly this was the last time I would be using them.

I had just finished an eventful fifteen months in Kendal and was off to Chesterfield to be near friends and have a social life. I also wanted a place big enough so that my grandchildren could come and stop with me. Or so I thought! I'd really missed them over the past year.

Seven months later.

October 18th 2019

Chesterfield - Decision day!

Today I woke up with a sense of calm. I finally get to know what is happening to me. There is only two ways to go. Either I am mad or depressed. Either option, Dementia could be a death sentence or Anxiety & Depression that needs secondary trauma therapy that could takes three to six years to unlock all the traumas I have locked away in my brain for over sixty years frightens me. I've been in limbo trying to consider how I will cope with either for the last two months. This has created many Dark moments.

Trying to come to terms with the above and my already assisted living from generosity of friends and family to help in my survival journey and facing up to the fact that my already fractured independence is in real danger I want it all over and done with.

Driving and having a car had always been my pride and joy. It gave me the ability to take the Grandchildren on adventures and have well paid jobs. This all feels like its crashing down on me now. My inability to remember things I've done in the last few moments scares me. The lack of financial support and extreme anxiety I experience to the smallest of things when I'm driving led me to get rid of my car. That day was a sad day but an honest one.

My inability to walk far and my reaction to people in taxis, buses and on the street makes my ability to venture out an extremely scary experience.

Today at 10.00am, Lina came to collect me to drop me at the doctor's surgery.

After my compulsory cigarette to get myself together and prepared for the waiting room full of people. I talk to my brain and agree that I must hold myself together and I go.

The queue is long and immediately raises my wonderful chemicals to make me feel hot and bothered. I breathe; long deep breathes and proceeded to the check-in machine to see if it was working. (It had good days and bad days) Today I was in luck. I pressed the date of birth info and sex and there it is my appointment with Dr A. in room 19 upstairs. Brilliant! For once technology had done me proud.

As I came out of the lift, I walked into someone I had recently been thinking about. Sat in the waiting room was Billy, an old friend from the past. I hadn't seen him for over twenty years. He looked younger than ever. Easily ten years older than me his skin looked so smooth and amazingly. I had to look twice to make sure I had the right person.

Sitting next to him I said,

"You don't know who I am? Do you?"

Billy looked at me twice before it registered.

"Veronica, Steve's girlfriend."

Billy said it as if he wasn't sure.

I blurted out, without thinking.

"I never thought you would still be around."

I could have bitten my lip. No bloody tact whatsoever. I felt a little nervous.

What possessed me to say this?

So bloody rude! Veronica engage your brain.

I then got up to go to my appointment completely embarrassed. I really have lost all social skills at present.

Dr A. was waiting for me in the corridor as soon as my name came on the television screen to go to room 19 to hear my fate. Dr A. asked me if I minded having a student in for the consultation. Having said yes before and feeling I could hold myself together this time I cheerfully said yes.

The conclusion of all the blood tests, brain MRI and various psychology reports showed that I didn't have the death sentence. Which was a massive relief, Dementia would have devastated me. But the brain scan did show that I was unable to concentrate on two conversations at the same time and understand what were said. This was causing the anxiety and depression and could not be treated by tablets. Rest was the only answer. I had totally pushed myself to the limit.

I felt like that was what I was doing sitting trying to focus at the garden, titivating the weeds and knocking my back up. How much bloody rest does a brain need? The medication I was on was the maximum dose they could give me along with the tablets to calm the palpitations. The remainder of the cure was rest and therapy which wasn't being funded currently. Even though we hear everywhere how much help is out there for people with mental health issues. Not if it's complex trauma. Useful.

October 20th 2019

Chesterfield

Today will be a real Challenge for me, to see how my brain and body reacts to a social occasion. It's Lina's 60th and I really want to be there to celebrate this with my second family. The

31

Palermo's. I haven't really shown my face anywhere much for a good few month. I've just been wallowing in The Darkness, letting the hat visit me whenever it felt the need.

Having had a restless night with extraordinarily little sleep it's going to be a test of endurance and a good make-up job. Thank God for Estee Lauder and Chanel. You're my saviours.

After yesterday's results my brain has been working overtime. I tried three times to relax and go back to sleep. I played over and over how I should tell my son and my family what comes next or not as the case maybe. I couldn't find the words or courage if I'm honest to tell Che and Chloe. I don't want them carrying my burden. It's bad enough I don't have the ability to see them as much as I would like too. I need to find a positive way to tell them.

I decided, as I have all my life to protect them. I decided to shove the burden into my brains cupboard and tackling it after the weekend. Kurt was coming and I wanted to enjoy my time with him. He really did intrigue me. I was eager to spend more time with him.

I finally got up after all the tossing and turning to dye my hair. I wanted to look my best, too much grey. My hair needed dying weeks ago. I haven't had the money, desire or need for it to look good for the last few weeks. Let's face it no one was going to see me. (Only those friends who were helping me to survive life)

I had decided that it requires too much energy to arrange to go and buy the £2.00 hair dye I needed and do it myself. I really had to feel good to go on such an adventure. My foot really was trying to show me who the boss is!

Thankfully, Lina and Anna took me shopping yesterday so I have no excuse. The party was a wonderful family and friends party. Organised as a surprise party by her children and sister beautifully with every detail being perfectly executed and thought of.

Kurt and I sat outside as it was a beautiful sunny day. The seating outside Maison Mes Amis, (The house of my friends) a beautiful French restaurant in Chesterfield which enabled me to smoke myself stupid and get pissed on Prosecco. Totally hiding the Dark hat when it tried to unnerve me. I introduced Kurt to friends who hadn't met him before as it was a fairly new relationship and he really seemed to enjoy everyone's company.

We did stay longer than I had expected but finally exhaustion hit and at five when everyone was heading to go to a few pubs on Brampton I had to admit defeat. A visit to the Union Jack fish and chips was the order of the night. Not that there hadn't been enough food, but Kurt and I were foodies and a massive freshly cooked Fish and Chips and a couple of drinks at home with our Pyjamas (PJ's) on was our idea of heaven.

Chapter 7

The Dark Hat doles out its punishment!

The Unresponsive One! (UO)

Today, after Lina's Birthday celebration I am a totally different human being. Some people have massive hangovers after a reasonable session. Not me, I have a, 'Massive tired over.'

Mass exhaustion isn't the word for how I am feeling. I feel like I haven't slept for days. I am like jelly, like a floppy rag doll, just walking down the stairs completely wipes me out. I have to force my body to do it. I need to sit and rest at the bottom. Anyone would think I'd just come down a mountain! What sort of shit is this? Ok so I broke the 'rest routine' and dared to go out and talk to people. I didn't upset anyone. I behaved well and this is my punishment.

The Dark Hat has completed covered my brain and is trying to stretch it to my kneecaps. If this is what depression does for you, I really don't want it. I'm staggered at how little energy I have. I can hardly move my feet. My brain isn't responding to what I am telling it to do. No signals are getting through. This is some scary s..t. I don't like it.

I never appreciated how automatically my body worked before. You put, one foot in front of another, and the body starts walking. Well doesn't it? I never needed to think about it before. Or question it; it just happened when I got up. Now I'm waiting for my body to get the message. Seriously, it's like a time delay.

"Bloody move, body parts, will you?" Impatience, sets in. (That's my internal voice talking to my brain) No response. It feels like I have hit the wrong key on the keyboard, and I am repeating it because I didn't hit it hard enough the first time. (Old keyboards need a stronger strike)

So now I have to talk to my brain to coax it and say,

"Come on let's do it."

"Wake up, I need to move".

No response! Horrible!! Absolutely horrible that's how it feels. Is there any wonder I told the doctor; I'm scared they might take me away if I don't get better? What am I supposed to do? When the body doesn't do the things you want it to it's like there's two of you.

Me, the one trying to get back on the right side of the track and this other! This other me, I am lost for what to call it. The Unresponsive One, (UO)! Who, just thinks,

"f..k you. In my own time! If you don't mind?"

Or in my Brain Language, starts to talk back? Seriously? who's does that? All the prickles in the left side of my brain disturb and worry me. They just keep sending some code message to me. I don't speak Brain language (BL). Maybe that is the problem. I need to decode the message.

I go and sit down outside with a cigarette. I feel uncomfortable I know I need to go back to bed and lay down. The exhaustion is overwhelming. I don't want Kurt to see me at my worst. I am so disappointed in myself. My exhaustion will ruin our planned day.

I somehow prepare the chicken for dinner by stuffing it with raw quartered onion and apple and just about get it into the oven, without it sliding off the pan, and then head back to bed. God bless Kurt he is so easy going he just says fine. He's happy to sit and chill in front of the TV.

Chapter 8

Flying Chicken.

October 30th 2019

Retford 7.00am.

OMG not again! I wake up happy. Yes, happy smiling. I am at Kurt having a coffee with him before he goes off to work.

Kurt came to fetch me on Friday afternoon after he finished work. I've had a dark week at home after my Sunday night chicken dinner episode, of a sort. Nearly dropping the chicken off the platter and burning myself on the steam. I decided I was safer at Kurt's, so I've been staying at his for the past two days. I feel much calmer now. I've done a lot of resting.

I'm still tired from performing minor tasks but not feeling so hopeless. I am trying to deal with what my body is capable of now and its random reactions.

I've taken my tablets first thing after Sundays blow out at Kurt. Yes, I had a blow out at Kurt. I felt so guilty and horrible about what I'd said to him. I cried I couldn't believe I could be so cruel. I hugged him tight. He's been showing so much understanding for these past four months, how could I be so callous?

Bitchy, the meds don't seem to be keeping me quiet anymore. I often find myself needing to check what I say before I say it. I really need to watch what I say.

Anna my best friend has always said I do it sometimes and so does my son. Engaging my mouth before my brain! The more I think about my past the more I am starting to wonder just what made me who I really am. An angry outspoken person at times, was that me in times of anxiety? Is it my defence for rejection?

Kurt assured me it was fine. He wasn't upset by it. But I was so upset I couldn't stop the tears of frustration. Both, for my incessant need to have him want me sexually all the time and my ability to hurt him with such unnecessary cruel words.

It has become apparent to me, that Kurt too has issues from his past and is happy to be cuddled and loved without expecting too much else. I, of all people should be able to understand that. Why can't I just be happy with all his wonderful kindness, thoughtfulness, and friendship he brings to our relationship?

I am beginning to realise that I can't handle rejection of any kind. Whether it be, Job applications, lovers, people being disappointed in me, actually anything activates the prickly feeling. My Psychologist councillor told me, "None of this is my fault!" but if it isn't then what happened to taking responsibility for one's own life? She wanted it to be the one lesson I took away from my six sessions with her and to always remember it.

Were all the original lessons of family value I was given as a child all wrong? Did I misunderstand my parents' values? Oh, I am such a bloody mess. I really need to find a way to get this crap in my head sorted! God give me strength.

Four cigarettes and two coffees later starring at my garden and the many jobs awaiting me, I am shivering, and I still can't stop crying and feeling sorry for myself. I go into the living room and hugged Kurt and tell him how sorry I am and go upstairs to lay down for an hour the exhaustion has overwhelmed me again. I just lay there and cried and wrestled with my brain till I finally relaxed and take a small nap.

Since then I have tried to be calmer with my neediness. Knowing how much Kurt appreciates us cooking together and watching him enjoy a lovely meal, among the many things we do together. He too needs loving but in a different way. I should look forward to discovering that instead of comparing him to any other relationship I have had in the past. He's done nothing to deserve it.

Chapter 9

One small step!!
There is always tomorrow!

I am now trying to complete just one small task a day. This is the start of my self-help. If I can achieve one small job per day, I might be able to bring some positivity into my life, a sense of real achievement, however small. Pulling five small weeds out is better than starring at them and watching them grow.

Yesterday's mission (I have to call them missions. Targets sound too live or die for, too much pressure) was a visit to BM Bargains. This is a large store just around the corner from Kurt's flat just a short walk across the canal. It's on Carolgate in Retford, flat to walk to and only five minutes away. It's familiar to me. I've walked there many times and feel comfortable going there. The shop is never full of people and Tuesday is an even quieter day. Lots of benches and rails to stop at along the way. Great for anyone struggling.

I'd be happier with Kurt holding my hand and guiding me but know, I need to learn to do things alone. If I do it slowly and stop where the benches are to rest my back, I will regain some independence and get some much needed exercise.

Today's mission is to look for, you guessed it, bargains, for the twins ninth birthday on the ninth of November. A job, which in my past brain life, I would have been so confident at. I'd have been like a spring bunny jumping round with excitement looking at all the wonderful gifts in the children's toyshops that would light up my grand twin's faces when they open them.

These days, I take endless photos and seek advice from their parents and have a budget to stick too. Budget shopping requires energy, a bloody lot of energy and ingenuity. Firstly, I research who has a sale on and understanding the best deals. Then I have to balance the best way to go and buy the items using the least amount of energy and create the least anxiety. Thirdly should I buy collect from a shop or get them delivered? Decisions Decisions!

Armed with a wish list from Olivia and tips from her dad about Oliver's current favourite toys I start to explore the marketplace with 10 days to go. The research alone is exhausting.

All the toy shops have deals on at this time of the year. So I have to decide which shop has the best deal. Then there are deals within deals I could buy two for one in one shop but at a higher price or two for £20 in another shop and the list go on. I could do with an obligatory nap and two red pills after all that research. I am having palpitations before I even leave the house.

Just a thought! What is required is a comparison site. Why not? For people like me it would be a Godsend. Comparethetoy.com? Would be a blessing and save me so much energy. In its absence or maybe there is such a site I just haven't found it. I trawl the internet and seek advice from others.

Ok, so now I have to break, for my obligatory nap. All that staring at the internet really does exhaust me. So nap time it is. Two little red pills and two paracetamols should calm me down.

I go out like a light.

A couple of hours later I wake up refreshed blurry eyed and a little prickly headed. I get a large glass of water to level my blood pressure to keep me sane. I do drink a lot of water.

I take a slow careful shower until the dizziness and uncoordinated head movements subside; I get ready to go to BM Bargains. Feeling a little sick and anxious, I wander round the shop still a little lightheaded and imagine people think I'm a little drunk as I sway a little with no one to hold on to for stability. I go dizzy looking at the toys, some of which are carefully placed on the top shelf which I can't reach. Thoughtful, there are signs up saying ask for help. I wonder round looking for help. The shop feels so big. Instead of being delighted with the vast range of toys and gifts. I am completely overpowered. In the absence of a shop assistant, there is never one around when you need one.

I take photos and send them to Che, my son for a second opinion. He advises me to look for the two for twenty pounds ones and points out which toys the kids would like. Now that made life easier. So loaded up with all my shopping with no thought as to how I will get it home on the short walk I start my journey back. I stop at the first bench outside. They aren't heavy, I suspect more box than toy. This isn't going to work. I need to get them in a better balanced order. Why do toy bags never fit in shop bags? And bits stick out everywhere and knock your legs as you walk. Mission accomplished, difficult but achievable. All toys arrived at Kurt's in one piece. I dropped them on the bed in the spare room. Time for a well-deserved coffee and a rest. That's one big achievement for today!

Chapter 10

A Whoopsie moment!

October 31st 2019

The definition of a Whoopsie is fairly simple in my world. It's anything that just happens without me registering how! No warning! Just Whoopsie! I am so glad I stopped myself driving.

I had one, only once, about three years ago, when I was looking for a parking place near Che's house to drop something off. I was stress and anxious about god knows what. I just needed to edge forward very slowly to stop down the road slightly as there was nowhere to park near Che's.

Instead of stopping the car keeping going until it hit the bumper of the one in front. It was my one and only blameworthy accident, ever. Confused and somewhat dazed as to how it had happened, my, bit of an anxious state, heightened to be fair? But this tiny bang, which hardly left a scratch, really shook me.

That was three years prior and I really didn't connect it to my anxiety. I was far too staggered that I had actually hit a car.

Now, when such episodes occur, I do start to question how and why? The chicken dinner one really shocked me.

OMG how did that happen! A whole plate of chicken dinner with gravy and all its wonderful juices has just flown off the coffee table and all over me and Kurt's beautiful green wool rug.

Last night I was reminded that the Whoopsies moments were still with me in the worst possible way. After four hours of slowly cooking a chicken dinner for Kurt, of which I was incredibly pleased with the final result. It was all there! The roasters, mums' carrots with dill, creamy mash, green cabbage, and lovely homemade gravy were all cooked to perfection.

Yum! Yum! After all that effort and concentration to get it right I couldn't wait to try it. I was so tired after all that exertion I just wanted to enjoy it.

These things can only happen to me! I must be jinxed. Don't ask me how it happened. It was a, now you see me, now you don't moment. One minute I was enjoying the results of my labours, the next my dinner was a disaster area.

Kurt jumped up, helpful and understanding as always. I just started to pick the food up off my PJ's and Kurt's beautiful rug. It was hot and getting into my lovely fingernails. I don't think I realised what I was doing. Trying to save the rug was the priority for some mad reason in my head.

Originally thinking, once I save the dinner, putting it back on my plate, I would then continue eating it, I then realised what I'd done, wondering what I was thinking. My brain really is on another planet. Clean as we are at home. Eating food I had ingrained into my nails and picked up from the rug and carpet?

Disgusting, Seriously Disgusting, I worry myself at times! What worries me the most is I really don't know how it became a Whoopsie.

I remember enjoying my first mouthful of food, and then seeing it everywhere. That is so frightening! Frightening to know it could happen at any time without me having any warning.

I normally have extremely fast reflexes, but I can't put them into action if I'm not even aware that something is happening. What's next I wonder? I will soon be scared of doing anything if this carries on. What the bloody hell is going on now? Should I just lay in bed still and do nothing out of harm's way.

I am scared of myself. It's as if I've lost that part of time. Totally blank! I didn't faint or anything it's just a blank. It is so weird. Is this what the Psychologist meant when she said, keep safe, and that she thought I was at risk.

At 10.22 am the next day, I ring the Surgery. I am in panic mode. I'm going to see the twins at the weekend after next, for two days. I don't want to be a danger to them. If there is nothing wrong with my brain what is this? I've taken my tablets at 7.00am this morning. Why don't they help me? I feel sick to my stomach. Should I go back home and be near my Doctors? I really don't know what's best for me anymore. I'm struggling with life here, which is bad enough; I really don't want to be a decision maker as well.

I'm scared to go on the train home from Kurt's, after my last episode. It's an easy enough five minute flat straight walk from Kurt's. Manageable for me, if I take it at a slow pace in broad day light when there are other people around.

Last week when I left, I was being followed and stalked by a hoodie on a skateboard. It wasn't something I felt equipped to deal with. He kept circling me and stopping every time I did. In broad daylight he really didn't care. He could obviously see I was struggling with my bags. An opportunity to derail me was in the offering. Then I stopped and decided to wait for him to pass me. I figured I had a much better chance of defending myself stood still. Eventually he turned around and went the other way.

I carried on as fast as my poorly, ankle would let me. I was only halfway to the station when I hear him behind me again. The sound of the unforgettable skateboard scraping on the ground grates across my brain like sandpaper on metal. I want to scream at him. Piss off you B…..d!

Now I'm panicking. My chemicals are going crazy sending prickles to my brain endings. I want to touch them, but my hands are full. I need to reassure them we'll be ok. Why doesn't this weirdo just piss off and leave me alone. I prepared to bash him with my hand if he tries anything. If he thinks he can surprise me. I'm too highly charged.

I see a lady turning onto the street some way up ahead. Too far too help but close enough to see. Or is she an accomplice? The weirdo pulled back. I kept going. I was nearly at the crossing to the station when the weirdo decided to drive past me at speed. I shudder, I still have everything. No snatch and grab! What now? He slowed down and hung about outside the station door. So did I. I really didn't want him to know I was going to the platform over the bridge and how vulnerable I would be over there. It would be a long lonely walk. I was totally freaked out!

Finally, he speeds off along the left-hand side path outside Retford station. I snook into the station quickly and sit on a much welcome station bench for a few minutes. I am really stressed out. What's with these kids? I really need a rest. Its fifteen minutes until my train comes so I can take my time. It takes about five to walk to the other platform and across the bridge. Not an easy walk but the only one there is.

The station is completely empty, not a single soul in sight. It's like a ghost town. I am totally exhausted and spooked by this creep. I am tired and sweating but all the time totally on the alert to my left hand side. There is a car park on the left side, and I want to make sure he can't sneak in through a side entrance and will take me off my guard.

Jesus is this really happening to me or is my imagination totally escaping reality? Its,12.00pm broad daylight on a sunny day, is my imagination so completely terrified of people that it can create such feelings inside me? Or am I totally mad? What am I saying? I am officially mad. I hate it and I don't hate anything or anyone. But this is frightening me.

Surviving this is going to be difficult if not impossible if it gets worse.

When I finally arrive back in Chesterfield after a fraught journey, mostly of my own making it is such a relief. I explained everything to the receptionist at the surgery and ask to speak to my Doctor. He is the doctor who I go to most often for my Mental Health issues as he seems to have a wealth of knowledge in this area. He spots things about my health I never would have thought of. I really don't want to go through all my history again with someone else. He is busy all day with patients. I was asked if I can have an emergency call back from a different Doctor as I need to talk to someone. I am advised it would be Dr S. That's fine she is the first doctor here I signed up with so she will understand my anxiety.

Dr S. rang me within four minutes of me putting the phone down. It was a No ID call. I initially looked at with apprehension. My whole brain went prickly. It felt like my hair was being pulled through a cap with a crochet needle. Exactly like my hairdresser used to put on my head when I was having highlights over 20 years ago. Strange, how we make these similarities to events from our past life.

I answered the call and to my great relief it was Dr Spooner. She asked me if I was driving. I said no. I haven't for over three months I'm too scared too. She said I must make sure I don't do anything to endanger myself. No baths only walk in showers, only when someone is around. I should be with someone all the time in case I have another Whoopsie and make sure I keep my appointment with Doctor Ali on the 21st November. Useful, a little scary, I am not really sure how that left me feeling. I was left holding the phone wondering if I really had blanked it out or not. Do chicken dinners really fly off plates? Or did I lose a moment in time? I am still none the wiser.

Chapter 11

The Dark Hat is back
The B....d!
Tuesday November 5ᵗʰ 2019
Chesterfield-10.30am

Bonfire Night my favourite night of the year!

I have just got up and I can't even sit downstairs and enjoy my coffee and cigarette in peace. The tears are rolling down my face. The pain is relentless. My foot has been twitching all night fighting with the bed clothes. Why can't anyone understand how bad this is? If I take anymore paracetamols someone will find me one day having a beautiful painless sleep.....and I won't care anymore. My brain will be free.

My tears come in earnest now, full of sadness and despair. My life is useless. This is my second day on my own after spending over a week at Kurt's. I was so up for coming home and being able to do stuff and get organised.

After reading my Personal Independence Payment (PIP) report reply, it reads as though all this is in my imagination. How am I supposed to look after myself? I can hardly move; I can hardly think everything is overwhelming me. I stare at my garden and am so angry that I can't do the things I

51

need to, to make it beautiful and keep it neat. The list is endless. Why do I live here when I can't look after myself, never mind the house and garden? I love it so much. That's why. I love the space, the freedom and the quiet.

Tears are streaming down my face I can hardly write. I don't want to leave. It's my home. My things are around me. Is it time to admit defeat? The Dark Hat is really having fun with me today. It is covering my face so fully I can't see or think straight. A tear rolls off my face onto the keyboard, followed by another. They resemble rain drops they are coming so fast.

My darling neighbour has put a little note through my door to find out how I am. My heart is touched. Someone really cares. Now the tears become thunderclouds noisy and reckless.

6th November 20

More relentless Darkness

It is 7.00am - After a night of hell with my foot juddering relentlessly again. I take my tablets and rest in bed hoping the pain will piss off and let me sleep. Why doesn't anyone realise that this pain only adds to my depression. The more painful it is and less independent I am, the darker my thoughts become. This is not living this is sheer agony. The inability to look after and protect myself goes against all my survival instincts. I want to build a house with massive walls round it to keep me safe. Or live in a deep cave. Live is so cruel.

The next few weeks are hell on earth. My days are painful and relentless. I feel like a bottle of tablets rattling all the time. I sleep I rest. But nothing helps the pain. I'm climbing the walls. I have to write a reply letter to the PIP because the report doesn't represent the painful assessment

I went through with Cheryl. I nearly give up. I can't cope with anymore intrusion into my life. I am basically a private person who doesn't want her life exposed to others so graphically. Finally it is completed but it has taken so much out of me mentally it's unbelievable.

Cheryl has been a rock. Without her as the CA I never would have carried on. Their understanding was invaluable support. Having to explain to people how many problems you have even in the bathroom is close to degrading. It certainly heightens the depression as I am having, to admit how hard my life is when the Dark Hat hits and takes over my brain. It's a part of my world I would rather forget, for the short periods of time I get that are better. The pain that you are put through by government agencies to get so little help in return is difficult to get over at first. Thankfully, time is a great healer and I am determined to heal, however many hats I wear or tears I shed. Victory will be mine!

Friday November 8th 2019

Grand Twins Birthday weekend.

Truly, feeling as bad as I had been over the last few weeks I really shouldn't have gone. But me being me I couldn't miss their birthday. Having spent the last few days drawing blood with every word I wrote on the PIP mandatory reconciliation form; I needed to see the kids and get a cuddle. It was a truly painful and draining experience. So I trudged on the train from Chesterfield at five laden with all their presents and arrived three hours and two changes later totally exhausted. The bag lady arrives!

Chloe came round to stay with me at Che's house. It was prosecco time in a big way. When tablets don't work alcohol does only for a few hours but when teenage girls want to stay up and chat, I need to spend some time catching up with them.

So Chloe rang a takeaway and I got introduced to the pudding delivery service in Bolton. Chocolate Waffles with cream. Oh My God, they were big and naughty. Luckily, a couple of her friends came round to help us out. I was exhausted and off to bed at eleven. (It had nothing to do with the Prosecco I drank did it?) I had a feeling this visit was all going to be too much for me after the week I'd just had.

The following morning we got up showered and went to see the twins. Nine years old today!! Bless them they were so excited to see me. I just didn't have the energy for them. We had a wonderful few hour playing and watching films together then, The Dark hat came over so quickly, I didn't notice it until it had fully covered me.

It was bad, I had to go back to Che's house and take a nap once he was back from work. As soon as my head hit the pillow, I was out cold for three hours. Totally wiped out!

After a strong coffee and a cigarette the three grandchildren arrived and said they wanted to stay the night with me. Seriously guys!

Well why not? I really hadn't seen that much of them over the past few months. So we sorted some supper out and some treats. Nanny always has treats in her suitcases and picked a film we could all watch together and vegged in front of the television. It was lovely. I was handling it quite well. Then off to bed for the twins and Chloe and I stayed up and talked with one of her friends a little longer. Sadly, I had to bail out, too soon. I love spending time with my granddaughter, but I was totally shattered again bed was calling.

In the morning I had a complete meltdown in the conservatory not in front of the children. I cried buckets and buckets of tears. Obviously, my brain couldn't cope with all the kids talking and demanding at the same time. Don't get me wrong. Not for one minute were they being naughty. It was totally me. I was just mentally exhausted. I was feeling so inadequate and sad that I couldn't get down on the floor and play properly with the kids and my brain was worn out with practically nothing just kiddie banter. Thanks Dark Hat!

I did somehow pull myself together after about five cigarettes and as many strong coffees. Maybe even, once the meds had kicked in. I then hit the frying pan to make the kids their favourite eggie bread. At least I could manage that for them.

After breakfast was over, we sat and read and just chatted. It was so lovely to be with them, yet I was so sad I couldn't be the Nana I had always been to them. Jolly and full of adventures taking them everywhere. Still you have to be thankful for small mercies. When life dishes shit out at you there is always a small piece of a rainbow out there you just have to find it.

Kurt came to fetch me at three O'clock it was a great relief. I was totally exhausted. We called to say goodbye to Che and Kelly and stopped longer than expected. Che and Kurt were quite chatty. It was nearly an hour before I got in the car and dozed off instantly.

Chapter 12

The Constant Worrier.
December 25th 2019

My grand twins, Che and Kelly came to see me yesterday with little Athea, my great granddaughter. It was lovely to see them and share food together and opening presents. No Chloe which always sparks danger signs. As she's fifteen going on thirty she can be very spirited and more. Hopefully, she will come later on in the year to see me.

Am I a bit heartbroken? Yes but lovely to see all the little ones and if I'm honest tiring enough. Big hugs for all I haven't seen them since they gave me the Flu or whatever it was from my November visit. It was a lovely visit; I was so sad to see them all go even though I was shattered.

I often wonder how many people wake up like I do in the morning, restless and worried about the world and life. So much so that it keeps them awake even after the little red pills have been taken. Do other people with mental illnesses feel like I do? Or are we all different? Difficult to know if it's just me that obsesses to this degree and always has. I often feel like the great protector. I seem to be worrying about everyone but myself.

I feel the need to be assured my brood is safe and everyone gets to bed safely each night.

Will I always be like this? I am the worrier, the one who wakes up with the whole worlds worries on her shoulders, what a shitty gift to be burdened with? God, I hope not. I'd really like to wake

up happy and feel all was right and settled in the world. That the burden of life and its happiness had been passed on to someone else.

I really do wonder how many people wake up truly feeling like this. Dissatisfied misplaced, yet have a lovely family and friends? Talk about have your cake and eat it. Why can't I switch the right button on and reset myself? When I do think about my wonderful family, I smile a lot, but I also fear a lot for them too. Our world seems to be getting uglier by the day and I can't change it for them.

If there are truly so many people with mental illnesses and it's good to talk about it, then why don't I feel better? Because in all honesty, I don't, is it as my Psychologist suggests I need trauma therapy to unlock and ease this burden I am carrying.

I still cringe at the thought that I am not able to work because my brain won't let me and has had enough. I feel cheated, robbed I have so much more I wanted to do.

Chapter 13

Things that make me sweat
January 7th 2020
Chesterfield10.30am

I really can see where the title of this chapter might make people really think, do I want to know? Well if I'm being honest about helping others from my experiences it has to be warts and all. It's reminiscent of completing a PIP form. You are laid so completely bare that I feel others need to know that it's not just them who feel totally violated by the experience. I do too, so let's share.

Incidentally, I did finally manage to get my act together and go shopping yesterday. My anxiety attacked me chemically within a few minutes of entering the taxi. The taxi driver was adamant that he needed to play the Spanish inquisition. Would he stop? Nope, the sweat came in earnest. The more intrusive the questions became the more the sweat poured from every orifice it could. Not a pleasant way to be. But that's anxiety at its best. Ugly bewildering and indiscriminative. I felt like shit.

The sweat, just poured from my head and due to my lack of nicotine intake that day, I was struggling and that's what really drove me to complete my task, a lack of cigarettes. (Perhaps another good reason not to give up yet) Climbing the walls due to a lack of cigarettes can only be put off for so long. Then I push myself out as it will get to fingernail biting time. It seems to be the only thing that makes me leave the house.

So, yesterday became a doing day. When I returned from my shopping adventure with some much needed wash powder, I had no excuse left to sort out the pending piles of washing and ironing awaiting me. My kitchen was so full of ironing and crap that it really needed a tidy up before I could get to clean the floor. Well, that sounds like I have piles everywhere that's not exactly true. Evidence is only on the radiators, hanging from the doors, piles on the picnic basket and still more washing on the floor outside the washer. So yeh maybe it is bad. I blame the bad weather. Drying is always so much easier when the sunshine.

Who am I kidding? Living alone it's so easy to hide things and let things slide. There is no one to upset or who can motivate you into action. Sometimes a good thing for peace and quiet and sometimes a bad thing for motivate. The jury is out on that one. No one to answer to and no sense of responsibility suits me fine. I've had too many years of it thank you!

I can see piles of sweaters and vests from when Kurt and I came back from our Germany holiday, piles from when Kurt's family came over for dinner and I hid things randomly anywhere in the kitchen that would hide them. Draws, cubby holes, and on hangers in the drying cupboard nowhere was safe.

Not to mention on top of another ironing pile and the ironing board.

Ironing activates my sweat glands. I really can't say whether it's the motion of ironing, the standing, my foot movement or the lack of my ability to balance, but something actives those sweat glands like crazy. The sweat just pours off me I need to literally sit and rest between items. Good job I don't wear much at home only jogging pants and sweatshirts. Appropriately.

Moving on, more sweating experiences, wonderful! How do you explain things to the PIP assessment officer: without losing self-respect and coming out in a sweat? Simply you can't. Its

degrading to have to admit the things you can't do any more. Cruel even. The whole experience rips you in two whether it be face to face or over the phone. I am so frightened that they will not understand what I am trying to politely say. Whether it be about washing or toileting. I often wonder if they realise what an effect they have on truly depressed people.

Another very sweat inducing time is when I am feeling a little better and decide to do something. Today's task was putting the stew, I had made the other day, into the plastic containers for the freezer to keep me going with food when I don't want to go out shopping or simply can't. I really don't understand how the bloody hell I can get a prickly head from such a simple task.

Definition of a prickly head is normally the first stage of the Dark Hat creeping on. Firstly, the prickles come on the right side of my head then spread while I am moving around. It is the weirdest sensation. When I stop and rest it puts the breaks on. Then as soon as I get up again the sweat continues its journey down my forehead. Rest is the only answer.

Certain types of food and drink can start the sweating. Recognising which, and how it affects me is key in my journey to understand why I feel certain ways and how to correct the problems. The problem with Identifying them is that they behave so inconsistently.

Sometimes a hot cup of coffee in the morning will bring sweats on and until I have had two of them, I don't settle down. Yet, if I keep drinking coffee the sweats come back with a vengeance along with the lethargy and prickly head. I become a truly weird person. The Dark Hat creeps up on me and say's "hey stop drinking this or else?" such a wonderful bedfellow to have.

The Dark Hat does the same with alcohol. I enjoy a couple of glasses of wine or prosecco and the same happens. My head is full of the prickly monsters joining the Dark Hat on its mission. It makes me stop drinking however hard I try to get past it. I have to stop drinking for it to relieve its pressure. Good job I love water!

Unfortunately, carbohydrates have a similar effect. If I eat a mainly carbohydrate meal the heat in my body goes up considerably. It feels like my indigestive system is having an anxiety attack. Now you know where I get the weird bit from. How strange that one day a piece of toast can give you the sweats or a bowl of pasta and the next day it doesn't. Or should I say if I don't have carbohydrates for a few days and then I do the effect is never the same. Feels like the Dark Hat is slightly indecisive. Trying to fathom a way to beat this is really not going to be easy.

Getting caught short, a most embarrassing experience in whatever situation. Once I was waiting on the phone for someone to come back to me. After, waiting twenty eight minutes, the waiting went on and on, and I didn't want to lose my place in the queue. OMG suddenly my bowels decide they have to go. No, this really can't be happening. I just can't wait. Please hurry up and answer this bloody phone. I really don't want to hang up. I'll have to go through all this bloody waiting again.

The sweat starts dripping into my eyes. I place the phone on the windowsill in the bathroom. I didn't want it to slip out of my trouser pocket like the last one did straight into the toilet bowl after I had a wee in it. That could only happen to me. I sat down quickly as my bowel was desperate to empty. As the first poo came out it was long. It made an almighty plop into the toilet bowl. At that moment someone answered the phone. Seriously, I dithered. Had they heard the plop. OMG that was a long one, following close behind by another. I had to speak otherwise I would lose my place in the bloody queue. I answered hello. Praying they could not hear the background plop which followed my greeting as if on cue. It was just as loud as the first. I held my breathe. I really didn't know what to say. Then the final insult. My bowls decided to complete their toilet adventure with an enormous blast of wind.

Oh My God, seriously how am I supposed to explain this type of embarrassment and a complete loss of dignity to my Doctor. Never mind the person on the other end of the phone. Call ended. I couldn't brave it out!

It is just too much, funny now. I know. But at the time needless to say I had to put the phone down. I was bursting with laughter. I couldn't stop myself. My bowels were what they were. Overactive and impatient at the best of times. I can't control them. I am only grateful that I have a house with a downstairs toilet because I know if I had had to manoeuvre the stairs with my dicky foot the embarrassment would have been far greater.

Then I had the painful experience of cleaning myself which always resulted in pains under my right breast with the twisting and turning to ensure I was thoroughly clean. How the hell am I supposed to explain such an episode to the Doctors. I really don't want to say too much in case they send someone to help me do it. That would be the end. I really couldn't cope with that.

Shoot me! Please. In fact, I'll shoot me. I'm going to France to buy a gun. There is being Geriatric and being geriatric, but bum wiping is my job. It's not something I really want to share no matter how much it hurts. Unimaginable. There are somethings a person should struggle with to the very end and that is one I intend to.

I can always remember receiving a phone call from the nursing home my mother was in over 40 years ago. It utterly amazed me.

March 1976
Solihull Nursing home.

"Hi, is that Veronica," The Sister from my mother's nursing home rang me.

"Yes, who's that?" (At my flat in Chesterfield. Well a bedsit really, we had a phone in the hall we all shared. No mobile phones in those days.)

"It's the sister from your mothers nursing home. Can you talk?"

"Yes, what's wrong? Is Mother ok?"

"I need you to talk to her. She keeps insisting on walking to the toilet instead of having a commode at the side of the bed." (Was she serious?)

"Seriously, why, can't she go to the toilet? If she wants to?"

"She's too weak and fragile."

"So, walk with her and supervise." I replied, that's why she's there isn't it.

"She just keeps wondering off on her own."

"Well what do you want me to do? You're at the hospital I'm not."

"You need to tell her to stop doing it!" Given I get my determination from my mother, you can guess my response.

"Seriously! Me tell my mother she can't go to the toilet on her own if she wants to. Sorry, I have more respect than that. If my mother wants to retain her dignity and go to the toilet in the little girl's room down the hall then I suggest you find someone to help her walk there or keep an eye

on her. I would not presume to tell my mother she had to have a commode while she can still walk. I know what a proud woman she is. You would be stripping her of a scared dignity." I couldn't believe my ears.

"But you don't understand Veronica." The sister insisted.

"Oh, but I do. It's bad enough my father has had her moved from her home because he couldn't cope with her without telling any of us, and he's put her in an expensive nursing home with a load of strangers. Now you want me to tell her she can't go for a walk to the loo. Well I think that's what you guys there are for, to look after her. Not to keep her in bed if she is able to walk."

(Bear in mind I am a seventeen-year-old girl at this time, who ran away from home.) I really didn't want anyone making that phone call to my son.

How utterly embarrassing. Where was her sense of human dignity? Funny how things come around in life!

Chapter 14

Economical living!

9th January 2020

How difficult can it be to fill in a blue badge form? Well, for a person in full possession of their faculties it's like applying for a passport online. Which is smooth and seamless if you don't have anxiety and depression. For me this would be the first form I would attempt to complete without any help from Cheryl or the CA.

With anxiety and sweats it's another story. No wonder they give you seven days to complete and the ability to pause and save when you don't have all the information or have had enough of completing it.

I did try to call the Derbyshire County Council for advice but after twenty-eight minutes on the phone my nerves were torn to shreds. My brain was so bloody tired I wanted to scream. Having achieved extraordinarily little I didn't understand how I could be so massively exhausted. To the point I had to go to bed. My eyes couldn't stay open. I was anxious and so slow it had exhausted me so much. Being up from five thirty in the morning until eight at night trying to battle with this simple form had totally wiped me out. Off to bed I went.

10th January 2020

Yesterday, maybe I had spent too much time thinking about the form and how best to complete. My muddled mind sees problems that don't really exist. Today with a fresh brain the finishing touches were easy. It's unbelievable, how much trying to sort out my life on my own is taking out of me, mentally and physically. I must have built myself up to such an anxious frenzy

yesterday that I could not think straight. Anxiety does make for very strange bed fellows indeed. More worryingly it stops my body producing anything. Whether it be physical action or mental functioning. It decides to just pull the plug and stop me doing anything at all. I can get up to pick something up and instantly I have forgotten what it is. Will I ever be able to manage that switch back to some sort of normality? I really hope so, only time will tell. The more I observe about what is happening to me the more I wonder what my end state will be.

At least now, anyone who is kind enough to drive me, will be able to park near the door of the supermarket and save my feet and valuable energy for wandering around the store. One good economy measure given my current meagre budget. Previously I was having to pay for taxis or buss which are both expensive and anxiety triggers (AT). It was costing me upwards of ten pounds for a return journey and up to half an hour standing time when buses or taxis weren't available.

There are several ways to help balance the budget of a partially disabled person who can't actually work, like myself. (Due to mental or physical disability) This is a person who has time to get from A to B when they push themselves at their own pace, under no time constraints.

Once you acquire enough points on the PIP system you can apply for a bus pass in Derbyshire and many other areas of the UK. It's called a Gold Card. Anyone with eight points and over can apply.

The Gold Card isn't actually that difficult to attain. I went to the Chesterfield borough council offices to enquired about a form required to start the process. The information customer service desk was more than happy to help and took my photo for the pass to kick the process off and confirmed they had seen a copy of my proof of disability points. It wasn't my best time for photos as I had just had an anxious time going through council tax benefits which were mind boggling due to the number of letters I'd been sent by them, but it certainly speeded the process up. The lady gave me a form which required extraordinarily little filling in. I sent it off and within a week the pass arrived. I found this to be the most efficient process of all the benefits.

The bus passes arrival felt like total freedom. Wonderful how such a small thing can give so much pleasure. No more checking if I had enough cash to go to the shops on the bus. I could just decide I wanted to go somewhere when my brain felt able. Which is hugely different to planning a journey? As often when planning a journey, I would cancel the excursion because of a break down in my ability to move around or severe anxiousness.

The bus fares in my area can be rather high just to the shop and come back again as I would have to take a bus one way and a taxi to return. I could now even try going by bus to Kurt's to save him some time from collecting me every weekend. I had nothing else to do all day so I could put my energy into saving Kurt a couple of hours driving. Bless him he works so hard and never complains.

As the bus stop was right outside my house, I literally just had to walk across the road, two minutes before the bus's arrival time. Then when I get to Chesterfield, I would swap buses at the station which was no distance at all. It was all really easy and a lot less walking than from the station in Retford. (Although not far, for me it was.)

Having found a newfound free way to travel, I just needed to master my ability to sit for so long with people around me which given my current track record of social tolerance and unfounded fears I would need to work on a solution.

Finding ways to keep myself distracted while traveling with a book, a magazine or my notebook proved to be a good decision.

On my first adventure when I needed to swap bus at Worksop, I sat down for a rest in the station to wait for my connecting bus. Bad decision! A strange chap, strange because he appeared to be talking to himself, who had a lot of space around, which might account for my encounter with him.

As I took my seat, he started to talk to me about religion. I swear, I bloody attract them like flies. I must have a beacon on my head saying, "I'm hear feel free to unload, or Councillor V." I did look around me to check it was me he was talking to me. Fine! I thought, I can cope with this until the bus comes, thinking he'll soon dry up of conversation, if I put my head in a book and keep looking up and nodding, not to appear too rude.

But no, he was relentless and kept on and on about being saved by God. Everyone was looking at him and shaking their heads. I got the feeling they had heard it all before.

I smiled and got up when the bus came into the station. Heading for the front of the queue so that I could get on first. Not the kindest of attitudes, I know but I had to protect my sanity. After three versions of the same story I needed to protect my sanity. I found a seat at the back of the bus and put my shopping on the seat next to me so he couldn't sit next to me. Safe at last, maybe not!

He then decided to sit next to another woman right in front of me. The poor woman had to listen to him re tell the same story. To be fair I really did feel for him. The woman he sat next to clearly ignored him. He then began to raise his voice as he didn't feel she was listening to him I presume. From my point of view, fifth time round I am all God'd out! I really hope people don't see me that way when I get repetitive. Worrying!

Early days recycling – Charity Shops.

For many years now I've been one for looking in Charity shops and finding a bargain. Charity shops are always my first port for shopping.

This was first introduced to me by dear sweet Annie, a dear lifelong friend who died of Cancer over ten years ago.

Annie like myself was a single mother striving to bring up a child on her own while working in the corporate world. We instantly bonded in our early twenties when she came to visit Chesterfield from Birmingham to see a client business of Annie's I was a partner that firm at the time.

Our taste in fashion was often of our own design and not that of the current marketplace. We both had our own unique style and taste. (I still have, nothing has changed) Our love for clothes, we couldn't always afford the price tag of, given all our other responsibilities in life, led us on many a shopping adventure with a budget challenge.

On one of our first adventure days out Annie decided we should get a cheap train to Leicester and scour the Charity shops for men's silk shirts. (For us might I add.) Why men's? Well they seemed to have gone through a phase of wearing coloured pure silk shirts, ten years ago.(Yes pure silk, we only bought the quality stuff) They had the baggy longer look, I was trying to achieve and the quality and variety of colours was far more exciting than women's clothes were

at the time. I had a look which I wanted to wear requiring vests, jeans (In my slimmer days) and long baggy shirts. (Good quality different shirts) It was a great look but as always, when you decide what your own look should be current market trends and shops don't oblige. (Not then anyway).

To say Annie wore me out would be an understatement. Who'd have known Leicester was absolutely full of charity shops. Annie of course. Working, in marketing like myself at the time Annie was very artistic and always looking for some fabric to create something with. She was a

great inspiration to me over the many happy years that I'd had the pleasure of calling her my friend. I still miss our two am conversations and emails to this day. Our adventures are some of my fondest memories.

This particular adventure would have been in the 1990's. We trawled every single charity shop that day in Leicester. With many coffee breaks and some shops required a return visit due to indecision as we couldn't make our minds up or we had already bought our quota from that particular shop. Oh yes, we had a quota of how many we could buy from any one shop to eke our money out and a total for the day.

There was much playful banter as we searched through the sometimes smelly shops, we could have used a peg to save our noses inner lining. It was difficult to tell if the smell came from the clothes or the visitors to the shop. In the nineties, well off people didn't really go in charity shops in those days. Hence we were there.

Deodorant was sometimes taken out of our handbags and discreetly sprayed if the fumes became too much. This ignited much giggling between us and the shop assistances trying to

identify the culprits and source of the offending odours. (A tip never, follow the odour suspect into the changing room. A person with a gentle disposition could easily fainting or vomit)

Some visitors to these shops were in more need than we were of, a clean fresh new look. They were practically given their change of clothes to minimise their time in the shop by the assistant. Followed by a look of shock horror when the culprit then waltzed back into the changing room got changed, walked out like a Bobbie dazzler and left their old wardrobe behind. OMG that seriously was the last straw. Leaving their stench for someone else to deal with. We would stagger out of the shop in buckets of laughter.

Coffee and ciggy time were the order of the day, that really was the last straw. Endurance played a big part in this particular adventure. We needed to find somewhere outside in the fresh air to sit and detox. (and touch up on our own deodorant as a person felt really grotty after being in such a shop) Donated, clothes weren't washed and ironed like they are today.

Inevitably, both being women of impeccable taste and knowing what we wanted. It wasn't like going shopping to a chain store or boutique. Any items we found were one offs and often were to both our liking. This did sometimes, more than sometimes, cause some playful shop scrapping over said items. Saying we fought over some items would be a little strong.

Nearly! Best friends compromise. Or talk one another out of the suitability of the item so the other could have it? (Not sure it's really your colour? Do you think? Does it make you look pale? Or simply it would look better on me? And vice versa.) It was always in the name of fun.

On this occasion, we went home with many smelly carrier bags having thoroughly enjoyed ourselves and acquired a new wardrobe. (God knows what the people thought of us on the train.) I did see a lot of twitching noses.

I have to say, Leicester city centre was one of the best venues for such adventures in the 1990's we returned many times. Sadly, the prices have skyrocketed as the shops have recognised the value of their items.

It's good to see that now in the 2020's recycling is stronger and found in so many places. One such place being Morrison's Supermarkets. Where people bring their read paperbacks, DVD's CD's and put them on a bookcase for others to take and read. The shelf is accompanied by a small bucket close by for those who can afford to give a little to charity. For those who only have copper to spare

76

they would return will handfuls of their own read paperback books to cover their sense of guilt.

It's wonderful, when I am totally skint, and I know that spending seven or eight pounds is not in the budget but I have run out of paperbacks to read, I can still go and do my shopping or just go for a bus trip to Morrisons with bus pass in hand and a few books to swap or lose coppers I have put to one side and pick a book or two at my leisure. I bet your wondering why this need for paperback books is so important to me.

Well, here we go, when life is Dark, and sleep won't come no matter what I do to encourage it. A paperback book with reasonably sized print and a simple story as mildly complex exhausts my brain. Reading stops my mind whirling and exhausts my depression.

Below is a list of the ten things I have found that enhance my life when reading is possible.

10 ways a Paperback book can enhance a depressive's life.

1. Covert operations – Hiding from others.

2. Give you a sense of bravery. (Confidence)

3. Sleeping – essential for bedtime. Fill hours

4. No Sleeping Pill better - Exhaust

5. Make your brain work again -pleasure first, business later.

6. Distraction – story – life – beware!

7. Learn to relax again – me time – at home not on a plane.

8. It educates and promotes conversation when you're ready.

9. It's a good marker to show you how far your recovery is going.

10. I may not remember all that I have read but at least I've tried.

This practice was useful to me in my current economic state. When I was struggling to find paperbacks to read and couldn't afford to buy new ones, I was that person.

For those of you reading this wondering why a depressive like myself would be so reliant on paperback book reading I will enlighten. Life may take many things from you while you go through a mental illness and the ability to read and see clearly is one of them.

Here is an expansion of what I've worked out already and an explanation for some of my quirky points.

Covert Operations.

Reading is like a shield and we may not be aware of it but some of us use it as such. Even if we are not reading, we can appear to be. Just holding the book up in front of you on a train/bus stops people annoying you. Or more correctly stops you having anxiety attacks and hot sweats because someone is just passing the journey time with you and you can't cope.

Difficult to resolve but effective if the person is a genuine nuisance.

You can peep over the top of the book to see what's going on and control your safe zone. Make sure no one is intruding into it. Or hovering too close. A bag or magazine could be placed on the seat next to you if enemy is approaching. (only if there are lots of free seats)

Bravery and Confidence.

While reading you are allowing yourself to adjust to the change of environment you find yourself in. Or the seat you have no doubt carefully chosen upon entering the mode of transport.

First you sit there and huddle as close as you can to the window. After the initial fidgeting with bags and your stuff to decide what you want in the rack if there is one. Then you subconsciously unpick yourself from the cold window frame and relax. Shuffle into your seat properly. Stop breathing in to give you more distance. As your confidence grows you allow yourself to feel a bit securer within your new surroundings.

You might even talk to someone later. It is always possible.

Sleeping – Bed and fill the day.

Dependant on which stage of depression you're in would depend on how good or bad your sleeping patterns are. I'm currently nine months into my current episode hence the trips to Morrisons in search of books are as vital as anti-depressants. I have to have a book to read to get me to sleep.

Initially reading was not possible or travel. I would look at words and take nothing in. Very distressing, for an avid reader, but a great indicator of how poorly I had allowed myself to get. No interest in reading or ability to focus always tells me I need to close my eyes and rest or try meditation, it helps to fill the day.

Once my brain allows me to read again initially, I don't remember the story, so I find myself re reading parts. Memory loss is not useful when trying to read difficult plots. Tip (Try simple reading during the first part of your recovery journey) Whoops. Once you can remember what you've read it will help fill the hours slowly.

Beware however! I once nearly missed my stop on a train because I wasn't aware of how fast time passes.

No sleeping pills required.

Once I have mastered reading, I find I can master my sleeping and meditation. I read until my eyes are exhausted. This brings beautiful sleep. Peaceful sleep. Without the demon sleep full of unsolved thoughts and problems. Without the sleep of unexplainable terror dreams which leave me even more confused, anxious and sleepless.

The only downside is it's difficult to control initially simple reading or researching something on the internet, which still requires the brain to process is exhausting and can zonk you at any time of the day.

The trick is to use the reading at the right time, like just before bed to get the maximum out of it. (Hence, I always have a paperback at the side of the bed)

Make your brain work again

One tiny step at the time.

If you read until your eyes are drooping, sleep will come. More importantly if you read something light and pleasant (Or light fun as I call it) sleep will come more peace fully and easily.

Make sure the print is large enough and easy to see. Sharpness of print has a bearing on the eyes too. Even when I'm flicking though a potential book in the supermarket the first thing, I do is make sure the print is large and clear. There is nothing worse than squinting at the print with bad evening lighting. Read in a well lite area so that your eyes are relaxed and not straining.

Complexed reading however, as I learned the hard way (small tip) will continue to make your brain struggle to take things in. Your brain will need to be sharp. The more complex the plot the harder your brain has to work to understand it. Sleep will come eventually but can lead to confusion if the plot has to be reread, the brain may struggle, and the sleep won't be so peaceful.

Distraction.

Dependant on what is depressing you, (this is where your honestly and ability to recognise what is really causing you to feel so low) is required. A reading distraction can be of the greatest benefit.

If like me as a teenager, Mills & Boon was the light book of choice to feed a teenage girl's fanciful imagination. Being, both quick reading and attention capturing reading, it totally distracted me from my then traumatic childhood and hormones. After what I saw at home, I wanted to believe in love everlasting. The stories always had a happy ending so helped me to get my feelgood factor back into my life.

Hence, I found it is better to read something easy which makes you feel happy. Something which interests you but is simply written. A simple murder mystery, A

Victorian drama a short story or a magazine short story to begin with.

It is easy to make the mistake that to lose yourself in a complicated plot, a long epic or a story true to your life would distract you. But believe me if your depression is as Dark as mine initially was complex reading, finances or subjects close to your heart are the last thing your brain can unravel. I found when I tried to read such literature, I would have to read sections several times as my brain could not take it in. The distraction was causing me more harm than good.

Learn to have me time.

Making time to read and enjoy reading is vastly different to reading because you don't want to talk to people around you. I remember reading the Metro newspaper on the train, or tram to Manchester so that I didn't have to talk to anyone around me. The many flights I have boarded over my life were all with a book in hand to ensure I didn't have to talk to anyone while traveling.

The only time I really enjoy reading is on a beach in between sunbathing and going to bed early with one. These times are my times. Times I choose to read not times I had to read. These are truly relaxing times.

Educates and promotes
conversation.

Towards the latter part of my depression once the brain becomes receptive to reading the paperback book became an intricate part of my recovery mechanism. It opens up all sorts of possibilities. The more I read the more I want to, it becomes addictive, I have soon collected many topics to promote conversation with others and begin to feel able to offer something to the conversation.

This could be something I have read in a paperback, a newspaper, or in fact any publication. The worlds my oyster.

It's a good Marker!

My ability to read is an excellent marker of how far you have recovered. As I go up the ladder of reading from small items, jam jar labels to paper pack books, newspapers to complexed plots I see how fast I am improving. If I become confused again by plots and the complexity of a novel this is an alert that the tiredness is returning again, and I am possibly doing too much. It really is a good monitoring system. The longer my brain wants to read, the longer I know my concentration is alert and working again.

The end is much like the beginning. In the beginning when depression sneaks up on me, it starts to attack my concentration and I begin to nod at the strangest times. It takes me quite by surprised.

I remember sitting at my typewriter finishing my notes one day while working long hours in Cumbria and my head started to nod, like the old nodding dog that father used to have in front of his old Hillman car. It was so ugly yet so significant. Back and forth my head rocked until I woke myself up just like the dog on the window.

Usually that was a sign I needed to go home or to chill at the gym, but I always pushed myself to get more done. Usually leading to me going straight home to bed.

I may not remember all that I have read.

When it becomes difficult to remember what I have read I am either too tired, distracted or my mind is telling me to rest. The benefit is that I've tried, and my brain is trying to understand at which stage of recovery I am at.

At which ever point I am at in the paper back reading cycle it helps me to understand how to help myself.

I can now identify depression before I hit rock bottom, but you have to be aware of the triggers. Once I get to this stage, I know I'm getting slightly better. The Dark hat can be stopped from totally covering my head. But the key is I must listen to it and act in good time.

Chapter 15

The darkness if finally lifting.
After 9 months of perpetual darkness.

Eighteen months of driving myself over the edge with work, shaking and crying. It was time for this all to stop. This time I have to get it right. I can't go through this again. Too much Darkness, it nearly took me. Lessons must be learnt. Poverty and peace are fine I'll learn to live with it for my sanity.

11th January 2020
9.15 am Chesterfield

This morning I woke up and I felt different. I marvelled at the fact that something was different about me. I couldn't put my finger on it. I felt sunny and yes …happy. As if the darkness had lifted. I couldn't feel the Dark Hat. I touched my head, my ears, my eyes there was nothing there. It had gone.

I felt a little dizzy but no longer held down or being dragged to the ground and pinned to the floor. Lost and distracted. The Dark hat felt like the smallest beret on the top of my head. Not the heavy woollen burden I had been carrying for the last nine months, whose weight I couldn't bare as it made my eyes close and my brain tired and sleepy as if I were on some powerful drug.

Today was the first day of my new life. I didn't know it yet, but my brain was back. Still in its adolescence but definitely fighting to be back out there and do its stuff. My powers of thinking straight were slowly coming back. It was like a re birth. Being a child and learning things for the first time. A little at time.

Retford family night Thai Meal at Kurt's
18th January 2020 20.15 pm

After a week of self-discovery and finding my writing again, I was well and truly back in some small way. I felt as if my life had been given back to me and it felt so precious. Direction and purpose were all slotting back into place. It was a wonderful feeling.

Could I really be getting back to me old self of over two years ago. There had been no sign of The Dark Hat for a week. Just a little beret of tiredness when I did too much. My sleeping patterns were disturbed again. But only because I was able to do things and maybe I did a little too much.

Writing was exciting now it ran from my fingers at the speed of an intercity express train. I had to stop myself at times. I had so many stories in my head and suddenly I knew how to write them again. I had scraps of paper with notes on everywhere.

Thoughts and ideas came into my head at the most inconvenient times. I had to write them down for fear of forgetting them.

Yes, I wasn't out of the woods yet. I still forgot things, but I didn't care anymore. I knew it would take time for my whole brain to return and hopefully one day it would but for now I was happy with what I had. It gave me something I really thought I'd lost forever.

My gift was back and this time I would treasure it and nurture it into the absolute best of health. Even if it meant sleeping and not working and not being who I was before. A driven workaholic always striving to be the best. Instead I would be the best I could with what I had but in a timely fashion without the stress and anxiety. All that had to be repaired too. Mostly I would insist I got the help I was intitled to. I wouldn't just get up again and throw myself into the rat race again. I couldn't afford to fall back in the Darkness again. It had been too hard to come back from. I'd done it too many times in my 60 years.

My brain had warned me. Now was my time to listen and deal with it. I was disabled and a manic depressive. I was anxious and scarred of too many people and frightened of my own shadow because of my vulnerability but I would find a way to stay afloat this time. Hopefully through my writing. The sea of Darkness was too deep and too frightening. The way back too painful and uncertain. Truthfully one day I might not have the strength to make it back and that really scares the shit out of me.

I can do this. I've learned so much from this last journey. I just need to find a way to balance it all and survive. Time had shown me that I could live on extraordinarily little with the help of friends.

The past has a way of catching up with you when you least expect it too.

That evening we were just ordering out Thai meal when my phone started ringing. It was Kelly. That was never a good sign. Something was wrong.

Kurt's family have a lovely tradition whereby each one of the three of them has a dinner, BBQ or some sort of get together every few weeks. I organised one for the weekend 30th November to the 1st of December, to coincide with Chatsworth Christmas fair. We organised it that way as it was easier for everyone to stay overnight than to drive back after dinner and we had intended to go to the fair on the Sunday but due to the amount of rainfall over the past few days it was thought better not to attend.

The last time I was at Chatsworth to an outside fair in summer it was bad enough after days of torrential rain. The Christmas market was out size and even wellingtons wouldn't have saved us. It would have been horrific. It's barely possible to lift your boot out of the mud when the ground up there is wet. It would have made an awfully expensive mud bath. Rather than an enjoyable Christmas fair.

Kurt Suggested he treat us all to a massive breakfast at the Yondermann Café at Wardlow, which would be of interest to all as it was a massive biker's venue and the food was freshly cooked and amazing. So, after a late night we all tucked into a wonderful breakfast and chatted. The rain had put all the bikers off as well, but everyone enjoyed the memorabilia in the café.

It's a lovely family thing to do and this evening was for us to have a Thai Takeaway as we don't have much room in Kurt's flat for a dinner party nor a dinner table, for that so take away was the easiest option.

My phone call from Kelly, led to a series of phone calls to inform my son that his father had died. Someone I hadn't set eyes on for twenty five years. It was difficult but Che needed to be told in a gentle way. It was not a shock to him as he had received several texts for him to contact his cousins but had been so busy helping to balance the care for Kelly's mum as she had been so poorly.

Che decided that he didn't want to go to the funeral as the relationship with his father hadn't been the best. In fact, it had never been normal. Whenever he did want to talk to his father, he was never there for him. He said he would think about it, but he doubted he would go.

11ᵗʰ January 2020
9.15 am Chesterfield

This morning I woke up and I felt different. I marvelled at the fact that something was different about me. I couldn't put my finger on it. I felt sunny and yes …happy. As if the darkness had lifted. I couldn't feel the Dark Hat. I touched my head, my ears, my eyes there was nothing there. It had gone.

I felt a little dizzy but no longer held down or being dragged to the ground and pinned to the floor. Lost and distracted. The Dark hat felt like the smallest beret on the top of my head. Not the heavy woollen burden I had been carrying for the last nine months, whose weight I couldn't bare as it made my eyes close and my brain tired and sleepy as if I were on some powerful drug.

Today was the first day of my new life. I didn't know it yet, but my brain was back. Still in its adolescence but definitely fighting to be back out there and do its stuff. My powers of thinking straight were slowly coming back. It was like a re birth. Being a child and learning things for the first time. A little at time.

Retford family night Thai Meal at Kurt's

18th January 2020 20.15 pm

After a week of self-discovery and finding my writing again, I was well and truly back in some small way. I felt as if my life had been given back to me and it felt so precious. Direction and purpose were all slotting back into place. It was a wonderful feeling.

Could I really be getting back to me old self of over two years ago. There had been no sign of The Dark Hat for a week. Just a little beret of tiredness when I did too much. My sleeping patterns were disturbed again. But only because I was able to do things and maybe I did a little too much.

Writing was exciting now it ran from my fingers at the speed of an intercity express train. I had to stop myself at times. I had so many stories in my head and suddenly I knew how to write them again. I had scraps of paper with notes on everywhere. Thoughts and ideas came into my head at the most inconvenient times. I had to write them down for fear of forgetting them.

Yes, I wasn't out of the woods yet. I still forgot things, but I didn't care anymore. I knew it would take time for my whole brain to return and hopefully one day it would but for now I was happy with what I had. It gave me something I really thought I'd lost forever.

My gift was back and this time I would treasure it and nurture it into the absolute best of health. Even if it meant sleeping and not working and not being who I was before. A driven workaholic always striving to be the best. Instead I would be the best I could with what I had but in a timely fashion without the stress and anxiety. All that had to be repaired too. Mostly I would insist I got the help I was intitled to. I wouldn't just get up again and throw myself into the rat race again. I couldn't afford to fall back in the Darkness again. It had been too hard to come back from. I'd done it too many times in my 60 years.

My brain had warned me. Now was my time to listen and deal with it. I was disabled and a manic depressive. I was anxious and scarred of too many people and frightened of my own shadow because of my vulnerability but I would find a way to stay afloat this time. Hopefully through my writing. The sea of Darkness was too deep and too frightening. The way back too painful and uncertain. Truthfully one day I might not have the strength to make it back and that really scares the shit out of me.

I can do this. I've learned so much from this last journey. I just need to find a way to balance it all and survive. Time had shown me that I could live on extraordinarily little with the help of friends.

The past has a way of catching up with you when you least expect it too.

That evening we were just ordering out Thai meal when my phone started ringing. It was Kelly. That was never a good sign. Something was wrong.

Kurt's family have a lovely tradition whereby each one of the three of them has a dinner, BBQ or some sort of get together every few weeks. I organised one for the weekend 30th November to the 1st of December, to coincide with Chatsworth Christmas fair. We organised it that way as it was easier for everyone to stay overnight than to drive back after dinner and we had intended to go to the fair on the Sunday but due to the amount of rainfall over the past few days it was thought better not to attend.

The last time I was at Chatsworth to an outside fair in summer it was bad enough after days of torrential rain. The Christmas market was out size and even wellingtons wouldn't have saved us. It would have been horrific. It's barely possible to lift your boot out of the mud when the ground up there is wet. It would have made an awfully expensive mud bath. Rather than an enjoyable Christmas fair.

Kurt Suggested he treat us all to a massive breakfast at the Yondermann Café at Wardlow, which would be of interest to all as it was a massive biker's venue and the food was freshly cooked and amazing. So, after a late night we all tucked into a wonderful breakfast and chatted. The rain had put all the bikers off as well, but everyone enjoyed the memorabilia in the café.

It's a lovely family thing to do and this evening was for us to have a Thai Takeaway as we don't have much room in Kurt's flat for a dinner party nor a dinner table, for that so take away was the easiest option.

My phone call from Kelly, led to a series of phone calls to inform my son that his father had died. Someone I hadn't set eyes on for twenty five years. It was difficult but Che needed to be told in a gentle way. It was not a shock to him as he had received several texts for him to contact his cousins but had been so busy helping to balance the care for Kelly's mum and his children as she had been so poorly.

Che decided that he didn't want to go to the funeral as the relationship with his father hadn't been the best. In fact, it had never been normal. Whenever he did want to talk to his father, he was never there for him. Every time Che went to see him he either wouldn't answer the door or Ken had left instructions that he didn't want visitors. I think he only every managed to visit his father in his home once over all the years of trying. He said he would think about it, but he doubted he would go.

Chapter 16

Identifying Past Dark Hat Moments.

Kenneth Kelly's Funeral.

30th January 2020 7.00am. Chesterfield

Not something I was looking forward to attending but I knew it was always something I would need to do. Ken and I had fourteen traumatic years and split up as many times.

A schizophrenic drug dealer who took the wrong meds and I fell in love with him and had his child just after my mother had died. I thought I could help him as he had just lost his father also. But most of the damage had already been done long before I meet him.

Falling in the North Sea.

Spring 1980

Our relationship was extremely tempestuous. He turned out to be a very possessive jealous man. Traits I had been used to seeing from my father towards my mother. My life with him was hard and certainly deserves another full chapter in another book. My head isn't in the right place to do this now.

He tried to psychologically control me. He became worse once Che was born; he was so jealous that I loved my own child it wasn't natural. He was obsessed with my independence yet was constantly refusing to pay his own house bills. His ability to bring the Dark Hat to its peak many times during my time with him was numerous.

Ken went to work on the oil rigs off Aberdeen, as a welder, two weeks on one week off. This kind of left me in a pickle for someone to look after my baby. Che was only seven months old. At that time, I worked on a three shift system at a factory on Brampton as I couldn't cope with his lack of attention to housekeeping funds and paying bills.

Vivienne, my friend from our bedsit sharing days, covered my night shifts but wasn't able to cover days or afternoons as she worked days. I worked at Robinsons at the time as an inspectoress on the nappy production lines. Which basically meant that I had to inspect one in twelve nappies off the manufacturing belt line. This was to ensure that each nappy complied with our agreed specifications and didn't infringe Peaudouce's copyright.

The upside of my job was that when I found machine faults in the nappy measurements, I would have to blow the nappies off into the bin. Which was a massive black bin liner bag. As I had to ensure absolute specification perfection to the nearest millimetre, often many good nappies would go off as well as bad ones. No imperfect nappies were allowed to escape me as we were spot checked by Peaudouce's quality director from time to time. So, if a few good nappies were blown off into waste it was better than any bad ones getting past me.

Waste nappies were made available to staff for fifty pence a bin bag in those days. To pass security you had to have a receipt from the shift manager as proof of purchase. This was advantageous to a mother of a growing baby who had previously been on cloth nappies. It seriously reduced by workload and increased my sleep time.

Chapter 17

The Test.

On one of Kens trips to the North Sea his harness split while he was welding at the side of the rig in high winds. The accident left him in the North Sea for a dangerous amount of time as the helicopter rescue struggled to get to him. He was only just pulled out in time.

I found out from one of the men who worked with him a few days after he got back, in the pub. He never wanted to talk about it. This was the last straw. His behaviour was never the same again. His jealously of his own child became beyond believe. It was like my father with Peter all over again. I was living in a nightmare.

Lessons learnt.

3rd February 2020

Retford

Although the Darkness has lifted the pain has returned to my back, hips and ankles with a vengeance. God Bless my chemicals. Don't you just have to love them.

As one organ is enabled (My writing part of the brain) and its chemicals finally balance to allow the part of my brain which has been so Dark to write, for which I am dearly thankful. My pain chemicals which govern my foots ability to walk, go haywire.

Having recently returned from a flat, slow walk to Retford to buy a few things, I feel eighty years old. Completely exhausted, crippled bent over in pain and so stiff I have only just managed

to get up the few stairs to Kurt's flat. Having already had my quota of paracetamols for the day. I must resort to rest.

Having learned my lesson, the hard way I promised myself I don't ever want to return to wearing The Dark Hat again. I just can't imagine doing that to myself and the people around me ever again. This time I want to get better properly. Now that I have finally started to piece together the numerous periods when I was wearing the Dark Hat throughout my life I will not only learn to manage it but avoid, to the best of my ability, it's unique talent of attacking me when I am most vulnerable, with a full blown return.

I am a totally different person now. A happy funny loving person. I maybe stiff disabled and unable to do some of the things I love but the Dark Hat is a far worse burden to carry. I need to and I will, now start to plan how I will manage this situation and get the help I need.

Anxiety still lurks around my shoulder. Several times while walking through Retford I stopped and let people pass me. I am crazy I know. I cannot bear to hear footsteps behind me. I am frightened that someone will try and mug me. To steal my shopping or my handbag and I can't run to catch them and retrieve my things.

Yes, I'm insecure, my disability makes me so vulnerable. That needs to be at the top of my plan. How to overcome this vulnerability. Help is finally at hand. My meeting with the chap at Walton Hospital last week to review my options gave me hope. He will finally refer me to someone to discuss the physiological effects of the operation, accidents and abuse I have suffered since childhood. This combined with looking at the orthopaedic changes in my body should give both myself and the doctors the answers we need to get to produce the right plan to learn how to keep the Dark Hat away.

The Dark Hat management plan along with my own plan to earn money in a different way which incorporates the above should enable me to finance my life and my dreams. The last nine months of poverty and juggling my finances by robbing Peter to pay Paul, and cashing in small pension pots, needs to stop. I need some financial security as well.

The government holding back my pension, or should I say putting up my pension age from sixty to sixty six which is another five years has made things really difficult. Trying to get help from the benefits system is exceedingly difficult. The house I rent eats up every penny I get. Lovely though it is. I can't manage it. The garden is too big. The stairs are too steep. I need to be practical. Like selling my house one year ago and selling my luxurious money pit Mercedes four wheel drive car recently I need to look at an alternative way of pain free living.

Retford Bang!

4th February 2020

Unfortunately, yesterdays over excessive wanderings throughout Retford, to keep my writing habit alive has totally exhausted me and my foot. I expected the walk would help my thinking processes. Not so, my brain is totally exhausted from fighting the pain. I can't believe that a little bit of wandering up and down the Retford high street with rests in between can have caused such exhaustion. I'm bloody floored. This is the start of many tests I will need to go through to see what the balance is within me to keep writing.

I woke up this morning needing even more sleep than before. Having had a good night's sleep, I didn't expect to be so tired during the day. At 11.00am I find myself being unable to keep my eyes open. I am having to really forcing myself to concentrate on simple things. Nodding like the donkey that used to be so popular in the back of a car windows. Only this time the exhaustion is overwhelming again. I wonder if this is how the beginning of the Dark Hat starts to creep up on me. It could be the first sign it's coming back. It always started in the past when I was tired and dropping to sleep at work.

Summer 2000 Royal Mail Swindon

In 2000 I was sent to Swindon, which is a massive Royal Mail Logistics site. I was sent by the Logistics Director to run a project with his new business development team. It was to project manage, organise, train and integrate the new two man build team into a training programme to implement a recently won contract with Viking.

It was a massive undertaking and the beginning of a new leg of business into Logistics with mini hubs integrated into the whole Royal Mail network.

I worked from six am every morning. Driving from my hotel in the centre of Swindon to the site. They were long days with much to resolve and many people to appease and make happy all at once. Talk about juggling hundreds of balls up in the air.

As is often the case with many bright people that join a project team of this size there are many egos to balance. I prided myself on balance and preparation so each day could deliver as

much to the team as possible to arm them with as many tools for their forthcoming positions. Not so easy with some of the similar things in life like systems, decided to work against us.

It was especially harrowing as I lived in Bury at the time and the drive to Swindon on a Sunday evening took away part of my evenings down time. I did it gladly as my enthusiasm and drive were determined to ensure the success of the project. It all took its toll.

A sleep deprived, very exhausted woman who had been nodding in front of the computer by the end of the project I knew I needed a good rest. Before my next challenge. The project life of an implementation manager on such large scales is both exciting and fulfilling but I obviously didn't realise how much it took out of me.

I took myself off to Spain for three weeks rest in the sun and get lots of sleep. I really was completely exhausted from over work and driving. The holiday started with three solid days sleeping on the beach or in my bed and very little else. Maybe another s of the Dark Hat coming down to cover my head, that I just managed to catch in time.

Winter 2005 Royal Mail Chesterfield

Another occasion when I took over a massive Project from the Director of Assets in Chesterfield to implement the removal, training and positioning of new multi-functional, printing, faxing, scanning and copying machines throughout the 3000 plus sites all over Royal Mail was one where I remember the tiredness and the nodding dog head going during the endless board meetings I had to hold with customers and a particularly difficult supplier.

The project was given to me, incidentally because it was at a stale mate with the director because the suppliers delivery methods were not as quick, smooth and understanding of our network as he would have liked.

It was a project that would deliver the business a massive amount of revenue and delay was not an option. An Instant £1m saving once the initial implementation was completed and more annually. This was the case with every major project I worked on. I bought in many millions of savings to the business which I have to admit I enjoyed every one of them. Job satisfaction was always my driver.

Along with the job satisfaction came the enormous stress that goes with persuading hundreds of senior managers that the change is beneficial to us all. It was to bring our business up to the twenty first century as much of our site equipment was more than antiquated.

Back to today – 17.00pm

OMG, the pain has finally lifted along with the tiredness. The chemicals seem to have levelled again. I keep blinking to see if it's really gone. It's so amazing! I didn't expect it. I must have had my Dark Hat on there for a while because the feeling of it lifting is so unique and wonderful. I want to jump up and down when it lifts.

Definitely something to talk to the doctor about on my next appointment. Is it a sign to rest? Or should I try and battle through it. This time I rested and did things in tiny bits even finally tackled the wiry greys.

Long overdue. Like maybe six weeks. Not idleness before you say it. It's just one of the things that gives me anxiety attacks before I do it. Then when it's done, I feel great. So why do I keep putting it off. I really don't know. I've been dying my hair for the past ten years. Purely because I don't possess the patience to listen to the hairdressers many stories and the length of time it takes to get it finished. I can do it in thirty minutes and then shove it in a towel and let it dry on its own. I'm not a faffer.

I'm not sure what test I need to put in place to make myself aware of all the various signs that the Dark Hat gives out like scents or clues before it's inevitable approach. What I do know is that the more observations I make and information I collect the better chance I have of conquering it. The test will have to be an ongoing exercise. With all learning opportunities captured and analysed to help me move forward.

Chapter 18

How to Manage the Flying Dark Hats
5th February 2020 – Retford

Why do I call them the Flying Dark hats now? Well that's a good question? The Dark hats appear to be many. Different ones for different anxieties. They also fly in and out of my brain like flying saucers. Now you see me now you don't.

No darkness today!! I shake myself and look around. No, I can't see any Dark Hats lurking around. Yeh! … I woke up a little tired but that could have something to do with staying up and watching, Miami Vice. Far too late for our seven o'clock getting up time as Kurt still had one day left before his knee operation tomorrow. I've been keeping him company and need to be back tomorrow night when he returns from his operation.

Still feeling fine and smiling I plan my journey home to Chesterfield to check my mail. Eager to find a letter waiting for me re: my visit to the hospital to start my psychological treatment and start asking questions and learning to cope with the now flying Dark Hats, that have decided to come and go when they please. I need to fully understand what triggers them to come and how best to manage them. I really need to be able to start planning my days without causing them to keep sneaking back. I won't be beaten.

In the past I have ignored the tiredness signs many times. Instead, I would check my tablets to make sure I had taken them. Not for one minute naively, considering that the tiredness could have been from something else. It was a kind of denial.

I know that when missing a tablet or two it would make me feel dizzy and my coordination would start to wane. So really, I should have taken the time to analyse why I was feeling so tired constantly and logging it every time it happened. Like I am doing now. But hindsight is an amazing thing and when I am whizzing around at two hundred miles an hour it's difficult to stop myself. I am driven to get things done not find time to help myself.

In the past, I know when I had mentioned the tiredness in the past to the doctors, they just told me to rest. This ten minute appointment system implemented several years ago really wasn't long enough to get everything out you need to say when you felt depressed. I would often just ring up and explained how I felt and was told to increase my dosage of Venlafaxine until I was on the maximum dose of 225gms.

No other help was offered. Nor to be fair did I ask for it since I had initially gone through Cognitive Behaviour Therapy (CBT) which was given in 2000 but that just touched the tip of the ice burg. I still have the notes that go with it. I often wonder who that person was in complete denial who wrote them. I wasn't honest during this process. Constantly defending my x husband.

This time I have to heed the warnings and find out how best to proceed. If it be resting as it was before. So be it. I will rest

Chapter 19

Cognitive Behaviour Therapy what went wrong? 2000
How to understand the Dark Hat's

Honest is the key! Twenty years ago, depression was a dirty word, as was it in my mind. I went to the doctors to ask for a tonic. I said I was exhausted. The previous day I had parked my car up after visiting a customer's premises to discuss a business solution I had designed, and I noticed I kept forgetting things and slurring my words. I was not myself. I drove up the bypass out of the customers car park and had a nap. The exhaustion was now total. I went out cold for a few hours.

It wasn't the first time I'd done it. I was so tired I just zonked out. I couldn't even drive from Sheffield to Ainsworth where I lived. Some fifty miles. I drove to Anna's only 12 miles and downed half a bottle of vodka on an empty stomach to try and remove my thoughts of uselessness.

Then I decided to, or should I say insisted on walking, Jack, Anna's dog. Even with Anna's insistence that he didn't need to go.

I got as far as the river in Somersall park and Jack was trying to drag me down the bank. I knew

I couldn't let go of him. I would lose him, and it was totally dark. I was totally drunk. I'd

never find him again. Anna would kill me it was her baby. Jack dragged me and dragged me in pursuit of some tantalising smell he was following until I fell into the long grass and God knows what else. I prefer not to think about it.

I laid there holding on to Jack with his lead for dear life. Knowing I couldn't let go, otherwise we would both end up in the river. I just laid down in the long grass and wanted to sleep. I was so incredibly tired, and it felt so peaceful and comfy there. No phones, no one bothering. Just Jack needing me to get up the bank and help him get home. I don't know how long I laid there, it felt like I had a small nap.

Eventually Jack got me to the top of the bank. I'd like to say I got us to it. But that wouldn't be true. The small Yorkshire Terrier dog helped me and saved me from a complete disaster.

I got up shook myself pulled all the branches from my work clothes. Wonderful. I thought I looked normal and untainted. Not quite. I walked Jack back as if nothing had happened incredibly pleased with myself for salvaging the situation with a grin on my face. Relieved I hadn't ended up in the river. The reality was quite different.

As I walked through the door of Annas, a picture of innocence, Jack safely on his lead and eager to be back. Good job dogs can't speak. Or can they? I was greeted by angry relieved faces.

Karen and Anna were beside themselves ready to send out a search party I'd been out so long. They asked me where I'd been then started laughing. At first, I didn't understand why. I feigned surprise. Looking at them with surprised confused frown. How long had I been out there on the riverbank? Anna walked up to me to pull out twigs and bits of branches out of my hair and

pointed to my clothes. Not so innocent looking after all then. OMG I really looked like I had been dragged through a hedge backwards.

The game was up. I had to confess all. That I had decided to have a nap on the riverbank with the dog. That I felt happy there and comfortable. What a mess. I knew I needed help. The tiredness I felt on the riverbank was the same feeling I had before. The same feeling of tiredness I have now when the Dark Hat starts to cover my head. I had to admit there was something severally wrong with me. It wasn't just alcohol; it was my body finally relaxing and finding a safe place to rest. My mind feeling happy there.

There were many times in my early adult life when doctors had sort to help me with my then undiscovered condition. Easy to recognise now. Not something that was even hinted at when I was younger. Having lost many memories of my childhood due to a traumatic childhood and teenage years. It pleases me to be able to remember certain episodes that are coming back while writing this book and sharing my Darkness with you.

The Valium Experience.

July 1979

Chesterfield

Che was six weeks old.

My son Che was born six weeks before my father died. It had been a turbulent time for me. My Mother had died in April two years previously to that. I was still grieving her loss. At just twenty years old I felt very alone. Yet overjoyed at my amazing bundle of joy. He really was a treasure.

I didn't really know anyone who had brought up a baby. Four and five year olds, I had babysat for my friend Anita, but a tiny bundle of joy was something completely different. I didn't even know that babies wanted to be feed at night. The experience was new to me. Good job I was a fast learner.

Don't get me wrong, I did read up on things but must have missed the chapter on night time feeding. In fact, the whole every few hours feeding section.

Please don't think I wasn't interested in learning about children. I was. But with me working, earning money always took precedence. I worked in a factory until four weeks before Che was born. It was very tiring and when I got home, I slept a lot.

I attempted to attend classes at the health centre but after the first one I never went back. It could have been because one of my pregnant classmates decided to have an unfortunate epileptic fit while learning to do the breathing exercises. Having never been in contact with fitting before and not understanding that it wouldn't happen to everyone. It scared me.

So that was the end of my class attendance. I decided reading the literature would be less traumatic and more beneficial. I soon learnt the facts of baby life, when a nurse woke me up one night, in the hospital at two am to go tell me my son was crying.

I was stupid enough to ask her why he was crying at two o'clock in the morning. Something I laugh at now. (Being a grand mother of four.) But at the time it made the nurses realise I really hadn't got a clue. Which was true. Luckily the Ashgate Maternity home nurses were amazing and kept me there for two weeks to help me recover. They taught me so much and made me feel so at home I couldn't have asked for better support and a start in life for my son. I was a good pupil and learnt everything there was to learn about feeding bathing and picked up any hints and tips while spending the majority of my visit in the nursery. The nurses had to prize me out some days.

The rubber ring and salt baths helped me on my path to start looking for logical solutions in life. The simplest things are sometimes the easiest solutions. The rubber ring was the greatest invention for a woman or any person who had been through any sort of operation in their girlie/boys' region or bum. I can't tell you how amazing it felt to sit on a rubber ring that keeps the stitched area away from gaining contact with anything. Sitting and lying in bed would have been sheer agony without it. It really was my best friend for recovery.

Needless to say, this experience didn't encourage me to have any more children. Sadly, I never saw it as the beautiful experience I had expected.

The salt baths also really helped me to learn relaxation and the natural soothing of pain and discomfort along with simple disinfection of my wounds. Certainly, easier than trying to keep wiping down there alone, after having a baby. A bit messy. It was like sterilizing yourself. I was encouraged to have three to four a day. It really did the trick. I felt really clean and soothed.

After a few weeks of enjoying the euphoria of having a beautiful little bundle to love and look after, my father and his girlfriend came to visit for the day. It was unexpected and unannounced, but we dealt with it.

I hadn't seen my father for months. I was really shocked to see him coming around the corner of our house one Sunday afternoon. Announced, only by our very protective Alsatian Dog, Wolf, who greeted my father as he would anyone. Barking on top note and trying to get off his strong steel lead and eat him. I think my father had a bit of a shock. He told me to sort him out his friend was frightened. Really, I was frightened, he was visiting me! What did he want?

It was kind of difficult to deal with a woman flashing a massive diamond engagement ring at you who used to be my mums' friend so soon after mum's death and a man who was so abusive to his children. The salt was rubbed even deeper into my wounds, given that my mother's tiny thin wedding band wore out and snapped after years of wearing it and my father was too tight to buy her another. Talk about stick the dagger in.

Che was four weeks old. My father was the only member of my family who came to see my newborn son and it was the only time he saw him and held him. He died two weeks later.

I should have realised he was ill, when he struggled to eat his chicken at lunch time and asked for it to be shredded that something was vitally wrong. I did ask but he said he was fine. I didn't push him.

Frankly, I had enough on my plate listening to his intended babbling on about how they had bought a bungalow at the seaside and my dad had bought her son a new car. I wanted to puke.

Especially, given that he had sold the car he bought me when I refused to do back home after mum died.

Did neither of them have any idea how much pain they were putting me through, having recently come home from hospital. How much I would have loved to have shared this experience

with my own mother. I was dying inside. Nothing like rubbing in it. Luckily for Kath, that was her name she didn't know my father well enough to receive the brunt of his anger.

I received a phone call from the hospital in Birmingham where my father was being operated on two weeks later to tell me he was dead. No one told me he was even going in for an operation. There was no mention of it when he came to visit.

The hospital wanted a next of kin to come and sign so they could perform an autopsy on him as he had died in hospital. Given that my two brothers lived in Birmingham I couldn't understand why they hadn't done it and I was being asked.

Apparently, they had both refused and I was the only other person who could. Wonderful, they couldn't release the body until it had been done.

Only Andrew knew father was in hospital. My youngest brother. My father didn't want anyone else to know. Only Andrew and Kath. Great! He had only gone in for an investigation of the stomach. That was on the strict agreement that if they found the cause of his problems was cancer the same as our mum, he didn't want anything else doing. He'd watched his wife suffer enough over the years. When the surgeon opened him up, he was riddled with Cancer. Father had left it far too late.

At the young age of only sixty-two, the second world war had taken its toll. Raw eggs and garlic for breakfast every morning can't have helped. Although they were from his own chickens. I don't think we'll ever know now after so many years what really caused it.

What we do know is that my father died of pneumonia in a Birmingham hospital as a result of him pulling out his tubes which connected him to a machine in hospital when he woke up. Due to feeling hungry he got out his little suitcase which he had brought into the hospital with him and pulled out his Polish picnic, of brown bread, butter and Wurst (German / Polish Sausage) washed down with a drop of Polish Wodka. A complete rebel right to the end! God love him.

So, after my journey down to Birmingham on the train with my newborn son I went to sort all this out on my own, as Che's dad was away on the oil rigs. I was told that it would take four weeks before we could bury him, so I went back home. I had no desire to stay there for four weeks. To be honest I don't even remember his funeral. Only the fact that I had to go to Poland to bury his ashes as no one else wanted to.

So, after all that what do you do. You go to the doctors for some help. Coping was an issue. All alone with no support or understanding it was my only cause of action. Anita my friend came with me. What was my doctors answer? The one everyone got in those days. A bottle of Valium. Seriously, to a feeding mother. I had no idea what would happen next. I was lost and needed help to get me through this.

The doctor assured me that I would be fine. I did ask, not being familiar with any type of drugs what the effects would be.

Fine, I certainly wasn't that. I went to the pub to visit my sons godfather. It was a bad decision. A couple of lagers and a Valium to see if they would help me sort my head out. Well it did something.

I must have been all over the place. Dizzy, weird, God knows what, certainly incapable of being in control of myself or a baby consequently good entertainment for those in the pub. Anita took me home in a taxi after a few drinks put me to bed and sorted Che out. I was woken up several hours later by my sons crying for food. He was a hungry little man.

Feeling like real shit with extremely poor co-ordination the strangest head I'd ever had I performed my motherly duties and mother and son went back to bed to sleep it off.

The following day I revisited the doctor and gave him the tablets back. I told him that I didn't feel they were the answer as they left me incapable of looking after my son and that wasn't the answer. Given I was his only lifeline I had to take full responsibility of his care and couldn't be totally spaced out and incapable of looking after him.

That was the beginning of my long journey into survival. I knew from that moment in my life I would have to try and deal with what life threw at myself and my son and I would have to cope with it because that was the only way we would survive.

Chapter 20

Is Diazepam the answer?

1998

It was a great many years before I sort advice from a doctor again for controlling the Dark Hat. I managed to use alcohol and educating myself to get a good job to combat any feelings of anxiety. That doesn't mean the dark hat wasn't whizzing around my head often. It was I just tried to manage on my own. I had made a happy place for myself and job satisfaction and watching my son grow up helped me to hold it together. I only went to talk to the doctors when it started to interfere with my earning ability.

Unfortunately, this was after entering into a relationship with a Walter Mittie Character. The only man I ever married and thought I was madly in love with. No, that's not true. I was madly in love with him at the time. Or the image he had sold me of himself.

Not making any excuses, but I am. There comes a time in your life when you and everyone else wants you to be happy. Some advice to others don't! look too hard. Happiness will just come knocking on your door one day and because your so pleased to have found it you won't recognise a wolf in sheep's clothing. I didn't until three days after I got married. Too late then!

I missed all the warning signs even the one that sent me to the doctors asking for help because I was exhausted and couldn't sleep. I was also looking for help and advice. I was confused with my relationship. I didn't want to disbelieve his fanciful stories until it hit me like a massive bang, and all came crashing down.

Being proposed to on New Year's Eve was very romantic, but with no ring and the comments I don't want a long engagement I should have heard the first alarm bell. May be the Dark hat appears every time I need to review factors in my life and when I don't it decides to make me. I really don't know. I haven't worked that one out yet.

So back to the proposal. No ring appeared. No planning. No mention of it for months. Nothing! We just kept going out and he was taking advantage of my job traveling and executive lifestyle. But no plans were being made. We holidayed together, went to some social occasions together. He always came to mine. I never went to his house. One to always remember and question.

So, off I went to the doctors for advice. I was feeling anxious all the time. I didn't want to believe that my future husband was telling me little or even big porkies! My Doctor at the time, suggested I talk to my future husband about it, instead of being worried about upsetting the apple cart. I needed to clarify the situation in my head. Wise words.

My Doctor also felt that I needed some relaxation as I was working so hard and driving so many miles. He suggested diazepam to help me deal with things. Seriously, given only an exceptionally low dose it would help me to wind down, relax and address my lack of sleep. We did discuss my previous episode with Valium, and I was assured this was only a mild dose and if I needed more, I could double the dose. The side effects would not be as severe, particularly if I

only used it at night or at times when I was feeling particularly anxious. I could not use with alcohol.

This was the start of my journey into realising that I did need to relax and was trying to juggle too many balls in the air. Maybe I needed to review if I was the best judge of men.

There is no doubt in my mind that the diazepam does help me relax and float off to sleep. In fact, to this day I still have fond memories of how reassuring it can be. Conscious of how helpful it can be, there is nothing nicer than knowing you will float off to sleep and your palpitations will calm down. I am conscious too that they are addictive. Is there any wonder when they make you feel so good?

To be honest, they are my favourite medication to this day. That may sound bad but as addictive as I'm told they are I have always only used them as a contingency. Knowing that once I need more than a few I need to do something different. Like talk to the doctor again. Which would normally end with my Venlafaxine dose being heighted. The odd one I don't see as an issue. It's like using a relaxation tape but quicker and longer lasting

I think if they had not been addictive, they would have been my medication of choice but somehow know that deep down inside I needed the venlafaxine to keep my serotonin functioning.

Chapter 21

The Extended Pension
6th April 2019

Why, why, why? Did the bloody government have to change the pension age?

After years of planning to retire at sixty to enjoy an easier stress-free life. It's ironic that the government has decided that I must now work until I am sixty-six.

After ten years of collecting my Royal Mail pension, which has barely kept me going along with a change of career to be a Personal Assistant (PA) to fill my income gap. I was really looking forward to the additional pension from our beloved government which would have given me enough to live on. I still would have looked for work to fill the gap, but I certainly wouldn't have driven myself to go after so many demanding jobs.

After working fifteen months to cover a maternity leave contract at one of the most intensive jobs I've ever had. Working for a health products organisation. Organising trips for surgeons and nurses all around the world. Along with all the other PA duties of a demanding Managing Director and Sales Director I was pooped!

Organising their many three day monthly sales meetings and their logistics to get them all there. Often a very exhausting job which lots of negotiating to ensure the staff and my directors

got the best deals. I was totally exhausted. But I did enjoy every minute of it very much and was always well rewarded for my work. Not only for the lovely places I got to stay and work in but also, for a lot of the valuable experience and lessons I learned while I was there.

If it is to be my last job now that I am addressing my mental illness, I will always think fondly of my time there.

I have spent the last nine years working various jobs since my massive liver operation in 2011 to keep the funds flowing until my government pension came to fruition. Always with the comfort that having a maxed out government pension, I would be able to live somewhere cheaply and write the many stories I had endless notebooks full of my adventures.

I still don't understand the Governments logic behind the age increase. Oh, apologies I know the financial impacts to the treasury is enormous, silly me. Are we not allowed to enjoy our retirement years any longer? Just because people live longer now, do we have to work longer while others don't contribute to the system at all and expect the same benefit. Don't the government realise that we all have worked at different levels of stress which affect different parts of our body throughout our lives.

As I have found out to my detriment deferring getting wholly better or seeking much needed help because I was scared to admit that I had problems, as I was too driven to make money to support my son and various partners. While pushing everything else to one side, I was never looking after me, which has now hit me like a massive brick wall. Bang!

I have to wonder how much research was done by the government before they decided that an additional six years of work would be healthy for all sixty-year-old woman?

Questions like that always prompt me to find out more. My curiosity peaked; I decide to find out who is responsible for the financial crisis I find myself in. I've no doubt that there will be endless reports written to substantiate the reasons for moving my pension age up sixty-six. I am

interested to see if any of them took into consideration what happens if a high earning woman can no longer work and becomes ill. What happens if she is like me disabled unable to drive and her brain can no longer think and remember things that are required for her to continue to work an extra six years and what has been put in place if she can't?

After reading all sixty-two pages of," Increases in the State Pension age for women born in the 1950's" Government Report, found in the house of commons library. I'm not sure if I am anymore the wiser. I am certainly exhausted and need to now sleep.

The Pensions Act of 1995 provided for the State Pension Age (SPA) for women to increase from sixty to sixty-five over a period April 2010 to 2020. Kind of a fast sudden move. What ever happened to incremental implementation or don't we consider that anymore.

The Pensions Act 2011 was legislated by government to accelerate the latter part of the 2011 timetable. Starting in April 2016 when women's SPA was 63 so that it reached 65 in November 2018 at which point, they wanted to rise the pension age for women to 66 by October 2020. The governments initial intention was that the equalised SPA would then rise to 66 by April 2020. However, because of the short notice to some women, given the significant increases the government made concessions in the legislation's final stages.

The changes gave rise to a long standing campaign, (back to 60) by Woman Against State Pension Inequality (WASPI) with some women born in the 1950's arguing they had been hit particularly hard, with a lack of appropriate notification to make provision for the changes.

The government debated the argument and decided that any financial recompense would create inequality between men and women and cause," younger people to bear a greater share of the cost of the pensions system", "which would be unfair and undermine the principle of inter-generational fairness that is integrated to state pensions reforms".

129

On 3rd of October 2019, the High Court gave judgement on the claim for judicial review brought by the, BacktoSixty Campaign. The claimants' grounds were that the mechanisms chosen to implement the increases in the pension age discriminated on grounds of age and/or sex. They also sought judicial review of the government's "alleged failure to inform them of the changes." However, the court dismissed the claim on all grounds (Delve and Glynn v SSWP – media summary).

The DWP welcomed the judgement. I bet they did. Anyone would think it was their money.

The Backto60 Campaign applied for leave to appeal to the High Court. This was refused on 10th November 2019. Its legal team have now received notification from the Parliamentary and Health Service Ombudsman (PHSO) that they will proceed with a revised proposal to investigate six sample Complaints of Maladministration. The PHSO are not accepting any new cases at this stage.

On the 18th January 2020, the appeal lodged by the backto60 Campaign regarding their Judicial Review about age and sex discrimination was approved. It must be heard by 25th February 2021.

Probably not soon enough to help people like me at present but good to see that there are people out there trying to help other people like me who are mentally and financially burdened from this pension change. This is the first piece of research

I have found that makes me realise that I am certainly not alone.

The only problem I'm finding with doing this research, interesting as it is. I become overwhelmed with tiredness. It must be done in small chunks which annoys me at times. But if this is the only way to achieve my writing, I need to learn to pace myself. As difficult as this is for my driven personality, I try hard to manage my frustrations. Therefore, I am not pushing myself too far as I feel this can aid in my recovery. This often means that the targets I set myself don't get met. Maybe slowly is best. I'm no use with the Dark Hat on as I know from past months experience.

My next area of research is to scour all the articles written on, was current mental health percentages of senior men and women over 60. The potential impact of them working longer and effects on their health and Mental abilities. I wanted to understand if anyone had brought a credible argument to the table to address the likely hood of peoples, not just women's, mental health deteriorating, due to the longer they had to work.

Not just in the mental health arena because of years of performing stressful jobs but also, how their body parts were affected by i.e. fingers, legs, lungs, hips etc. I looked at different areas to research to see how much was factually written about these areas to help the government make a more informed decision on increasing the pension age

Chapter 22

The effects on aging Body Parts of the over sixties.

People, all reach the age of retirement in different states of Mental and Physical health. That in this day's world is inevitable. Years ago, we worked in coalmines, steelworks, mills, factories, stayed at home looking after whole generational families, did endless jobs because we had to or because they were our only option geographically.

A better education system and a thirst to learn and better one's self, enabled us to decide what we wanted to choose as a career. We all thought the life we were choosing would give us job satisfaction and a sustainable family life until out retirement. None of us ever expected, that as a result of our, working lives we would engage other devils that would attack our bodies and minds in the future. How could we? Earning a good living wage, was living the dream wasn't it?

Most working environments have changed for the better. People are protected better and everyone works towards a work life balance. So why then would extending the pension age prove to cause seniors so many problems in later life when they wanted to follow the dreams and plans for their retirement, they had worked so hard for.

I wanted to review a couple,

Mental Health.

How many of us just like myself frowned on mental health issues and dismissed the fact that we were working too hard and too many hours to prove we were the best at what we did. While, fighting inequality in the workplace, unions, managers who didn't understand their workforce to balance the working environment, we brush potential health issues aside. How many of us had to work to survive because we saw benefits were for others who needed them and put of any hint of illness off as a minor irritation. Work and earning money were the answer to survival and the things our family needed. We were a driven generation.

Opportunities to advance came through extra learning. More time spent inadvertently working after hours. Relationship and family trauma were dealt with. Bulling at work was cried about and forgotten. Put away in a mental cupboard to enable us to continue to work. My belief that it would always "come to those who wait", laid strongly in the upmost of my mind. To some

justice was done through their own down fall. To others their cruelty and lack of true managerial skills was endured. It was a different world then.

I never saw how events in my life would affect my senior years. How relationships I had endured would tarnish my ability to think in the years to come.

When your brain is your power. It's sharpness your best asset. It is a precious commodity. Its ability to retain data and information was your prize. Once mental illness takes that prize away through overwork, unaddressed trauma, or endless years of battling depression it is hard to regain.

To help understand my thinking I researched health reports.

The World Health Organisation (WHO) reported on 12th December 2017

"The world's population is aging rapidly. Over 20% of adults aged 60 and over suffer from a mental or neurological disorder and 6.6% of all disability among people over 60 years is attributed to mental and neurological disorders."

There is also evidence that some natural body changes associated with aging may increase a person's risk of experiencing depression. Recent studies suggest that lower concentration of folate (a B-vitamin) in the blood and nervous system may contribute to depression, mental impairment and dementia.

The fact that ESA and JSA/UC figures for the women over sixty, rose last year to over 100,000 tends to show that there are figures to substantiate illnesses in this age group. If the figures are correct. Which I doubt as many single women like myself would never claim or admit to needing help.

Some could possibly, be able to stay at home due to others means of support. They could have husbands, partners, wives. They could have very few outgoings and are able to manage on what they have. (source DWP Stat-xplore. Extract date:12th December 2019. Over 560% increase)

Given that it is only a small percentage of woman which have increased the ESA and JSA/UC figures. The total saving (£29bn) the government is making by putting up the pension age, they should surely have a sum put aside to fund for those who are asking for help now after giving so much of their working life to this country over the past years. Not just chucking them aside when it suits the figures for a saving to the national budget.

There must be something put aside, instead of the hell that myself and others are going through trying to get help. Given I didn't seek help until I was advised to do so by my Doctor, and as time has shown just in the nick of time. Maybe our suicide rates would be lower. Who knows?

I dread to think what I would be like today if I hadn't listened to the Doctors advice. It's unimaginable. I am sure the State pressure to get a Job and lack of help from UC funding would have continued until something drastic happened to me.

Surely, if everyone was singing from the same hymn book. Linking government departments together to help people rather than sending them round the twist they wouldn't make people feel like they were begging for something they were begrudged from every department they come in contact with. And yes, we are made to feel this way. Please don't doubt it! It is bad enough having to ask for help, but when people look at you with that,

"I've heard it all before look."

You think, "You should see me on a good day. This is a shadow of my former self."

If it were not for organisations like the CAB (Citizens Advice bureau) I would never have been aware of what help was out there. Certainly, UC and the ESA people I dealt with didn't want to help. They just kept pushing and pushing me for nothing. By nothing I mean because of my meagre pension it was deemed I wasn't entitled to any help! Work that one out.

Physically demanding jobs.

An Age UK report from November 2016. Showed that women with physically demanding jobs were already concerned about how they would cope now that the SPA had changed. Six more years for Physically demanding jobs could have various health implications. The quality of someone's job seems to be a key enabling factor to a longer working life.

Understandably people who lift and carry heavy objects, people or packages can hold a different set of health problems than people who sits at a desk and concentrate without a break or drive hundreds of miles in a day.

As these come in so many varieties, below I have explored a few. I am by no means an expert. I'm just putting some logical thoughts out there.

Arthritis.

Arthritis comes in many different forms. The typist or data input clerk who is constantly typing and staring at the screen would have different health issues than the physically demanding working person. Their fingers are more prone to arthritis as are the data clerks. Their backs are bend over more if they don't sit in the correct sitting position. Their eyes are likely to need specs soon with all the detailed staring.

Yes, I know a good employer, or a good union would make sure that adequate breaks are taken. But come on, how many people really do? How many of us just sit there a bit longer to get something finished? I would call these, "the driven, just a minute people. who don't want to lose their thoughts?"

How many of us sit there and actually exercise our fingers to get a bit more work out of them? Apart from the fact that bunion type fingers start to look hideous, we would never notice the effect typing is having on our fingers or cramp from holding a phone for long conversations.

I don't know about anyone else but since I started using a computer for detailed work over thirty years ago. I've had my eyes tested every two years and yep you've guessed it. Every two years since I've needed new specs. I wasn't just ordering one pair either. One long sited, one short and sunglasses for driving. Not a cheap hobby. Believe me. I was so grateful when I was offered varifocals.

The only downside I found with wearing varifocals was that after a year and a half they needed changing. I did wonder if it was the opticians that was the issue. There did seem to be a difference in the quality of tests and completed varifocals in my experience.

I decided to try various different opticians. I tried most high street brands and private opticians when I was working in different parts of the country. Strangely, either the lenses needed changing more often or the frames started to break. No one was very keen to let you use a trusted old frame which had worked well for you in the past without charging a whacking surcharge of up to £100. Which never really made sense to me. But that said we do live in a very retail driven society which isn't always the best solution for the customer.

The true experience that really excelled in my eyes was a lovely Chinese lady optician I found in Tenerife, quite by accident. Sometimes stumbling on a poorly foot on the cracks of the pavement can really be beneficial to one's quest for the perfect optician.

I think, I have given a good flavour about some of the things that I feel the government could have helped us more with when increasing the retirement age.

Free specs, Physio for people with physically demanding jobs, free gyms and swimming from sixty there are many things that could have helped ease the burden of physically demanding jobs, Free gyms and swimming from sixty there are many things that could have helped ease the burden. Free cinema passes to encourage people to go out or reduced theatre tickets, events price reductions. It doesn't take much to make peoples burden lighter.

Someone to go to if the burden was too great. It's OK saying we've got all these organisations set up to help. I think to divert six weeks with a Phycologist to get you back to work and that's it? Only touches the tip of the iceberg for someone like me. Maybe a greater depth of thinking should have been applied before we made such drastic changes to people's lives.

Hotel Europa Villa Cortes

The Most accurate Specs ever!!

March 2016 - Tenerife

I swear! Somethings can only happen to me! My first day on holiday in the beautiful Sunshine after leaving a rain filled sky at home. I couldn't wait to go for a walk and enjoy the

sun beating down on me. As, always, the first thing you do when you arrive at your adventure's destination is to check out the place.

At first appearance it was everything I had expected and more. The entrance the reception its lovely grand rooms running off it, were lush and grandeur fit for a queen. Not often when a holiday advert says it's a five star hotel does it live up to its word.

This fabulous five star Hotel Villa Cortes located in the heart of Tenerife's most popular resort of Playa de las Americas on the islands sunny south coast was everything it promised to be and more. Our room was amazing with the thickest drapes and a beautiful balcony to sit on and enjoy the resorts pools, palm trees and see the wonderful fishermen in the sea.

The many shops, bars and restaurants on the resort's doorstep were known as the 'Golden Mile', the main resort strip. A beautiful flat walk along the sea front.

The beautiful, pools we saw from our spacious balcony were freshwater pools with a man-made fountain cave along which you could lay on the plush sunbeds and provided towels. The separate children's pool, and a selection of restaurants this paradise was complete.

The hotel was a peaceful oasis, where we could seclude ourselves from the world. The staff were there to ensure that everything was at our fingertips. So professional and courteous. Immaculately clean throughout nothing was too much to please its customers.

Initially I was put off booking it, as previous trips to the area, I had found too busy, but this was no mistake. This was the best booking I had ever made. Absolutely amazing.

As this was to be Bob's last holiday on this earth. (Unknown to us at the time) I was so glad it was such a luxurious place. He really deserved it for all his generosity towards me and others.

It's gardens and pools, a tunnel leading to the Spa and under the road to its own private chic beach were perfection.

The first class breakfast buffet advert was an understatement of the century! The buffet selection would please anyone from any nationality. The various types of freshly baked breads, croissants, cakes, pastries were from every kitchen in Europe and beyond. Endless homemade

jams, spreads, meats, cheeses all beautifully fresh. Replenished as fast as they are removed. A pancake chef was on alert to cook omelettes or any freshly cooked breakfast your heart desired.

A selection of fish, hot and cold, all to their own I suppose. Breakfast cereals of every variety with every fresh and dried fruit imaginable to go with it. Champagne and fresh juices to complement the food. Coffee so fresh and inviting of every flavour.

The piece de resistance is where you eat it. A beautiful indoor and outdoor terraced restaurant. Outdoors in the sun where we could eat a leisurely breakfast and enjoy every mouthful. The flowers and palms growing around the eating area gave me the feeling of being in my own special private garden. It really was hard to drag myself away. I loved every last morsel I eat there. So fresh and tasty...... and if I wanted to prolong my coffee pleasure I could take a coffee pot to the garden, Chesterfield sofas awaited you where you could smoke, without any one showing their displeasure or eat some cake or mini pastries or biscuits. Sheer idyllic paradise.

No wonder Jennifer Lopez enjoyed visiting here. Sorry, I have digressed but the opportunity to share my delight and happiness of being in this beautiful place overtook me.

Not too far from our beautiful hotel, one of my lenses fell out of my lovely new specs. Well, I say new they were just over a year old. Beautiful sturdy, Ralph Lauren specs I had treated myself to. I grappled on the floor trying to find the lens. Not so easy when you are as blind as a bat without them. Finally retrieved, I tried to put the lens back in. No joy there! The stubborn thing was having none of it. There was some stopping it going in and staying in place. I needed an expert to tighten it.

Luckily or coincidentally, we were just walking past an optician. A beautiful clean and very classy shop. As Bob gently push me towards the door, I was immediately welcomed and told that the problem could be easily resolved. Which was a great relief. The Chinese lady was a good salesperson.

She suggested that I have a free eye test as they had some special offers on for the beginning of the season and they weren't terribly busy. Bob being Bob suggested we might as well. I did say that we were only there for ten days, concerned that the glasses wouldn't be ready before we left.

No such problem, they would be ready in three days. Amazing, I was dubious, but she was so professional and helpful I went with the flow.

The examination was second to none. The lady was so thorough with everything and precise I was hugely impressed. It was a combination of all the good parts of all the optician's examinations I'd ever had in England.

The downside was that my varifocal new prescription was vastly different. Hence it was advisable for me to have a new pair made up. I some how felt this was coming. As it was such a high end shop, I expected the glasses and frames to be extremely expensive.

Bob said not to worry, to have them made as it would be a present for me, as I very often didn't allow him to buy me presents. I was persuaded. Especially when the beautiful Christian Dior ones were so reasonably prices. The price was unbelievable for varifocals and beautiful designer frames with all the things we would pay extra for at home being included. He paid in Euros less than we would pay in pounds at home and no charge for fixing the others. Which she replaced with the same Ralph Lauren frame as my frame was dodgy.

We went back three days later and true to the Chinese ladies, word they were ready. So elegant and beautiful. But the best was yet to come. I could see, I mean, really see. I was absolutely amazed how clearly and how smoothly the varifocal worked. It was like having my old eyes back. Well that was a first. They were the best pair I'd ever had! There's a lot to be said about making things in house.

I have often wished I could go back there every other year to have my glasses made.

Chapter 23

The sadness returns.

21st February 2020

What a brain! I really despair some days. What will it conjure up next? It's so inconsistent. Today, I think I just crave for my normality back. Whatever that is. Some order of mind if that makes sense. Instead of all these random thoughts and feelings I wake up with.

Just when I think things are beginning to settle down, I wake up with some new challenge attacking my senses and causing mass confusion. Today's wakeup challenge came down on me like a big thud of doubts and anxiety.

A niggly twinge shoots from the right side of my scull. It's as if my brain feels the need to communicate with me by prickly messages. I seem to need so much reassurance and love these days. Inevitable, I suppose, considering my current fragile mental condition and the fact that I'm in the process of making yet another house move.

My driven brain tells me that's fine you've done it before. It's no problem. You can do it!

My new resting body and mind, which is starting to feel the benefit of rest and what it brings to aid the workings of my mind and body is trying to tell me something else. The brain twinges shooting up the right side of my skull is like some kind of an early warning device. A white shooting star, hitting the brain and saying,

"reign it in. Learn from your chaotic past."

After 20 years of living in the same house in Ainsworth and being settled and near my family, in all honesty it was a massive relief to be settled.

Necessity of finances and the inability to get up and down the three sets of stairs led me to sell.

Now after eighteen months of living in hotel rooms and a noisy flat I can't seem to stay in one place for longer than a year. It feels like Déjà vu. I have awoken the wandering gypsy of my past. It's so reminiscent of my teenage years. My sense of being lost and what should do I do next is active in my brain cells again. Only this time my brain isn't in the right place to decide something, of this magnitude so I must take my time. Knowing how independent and difficult I can be living with someone.

This time my move is to Retford to Kurt's.

"Too soon?" my inner voice says,

"I wonder!" In our relationship of nine months?

"I don't think so."

Given that I'm practically at his flat most of the time and we do look after each other really well. Kurt stops me feeling down. He makes me feel safe which is really important at the moment. I really am sick of looking over my shoulder for demons from the past following. There aren't many people around who can make me feel that way or places.

Today I was supposed to attend the funeral of an ex's father. Someone who I had a lot of time for. But after much thought about self-preservation combined with my ex's words of,

"It would be nice if you could come and support Glynis and me." I have decided I really didn't want to open that door again. I know what people will say. I could shut that door if I did. But truthfully, I don't do funerals unless I really have to .....and I think that door was shut .

No, I know that door was shut years ago when we split up. As difficult as it was to do at the time. The split was easier to deal with because I found out my relationship was affecting my son while I was working away. Something I wish he'd have discussed it with me sooner.

Given that I really haven't heard or seen from these people in over 25 years I decided this door was better left shut.

Originally my move was prompted by the roof raining in over my bed in the house in Chesterfield where I was trying to settle. Andy and Donna whose house it was had decided to start rebuilding in April 2020.

Given that repairs would be a waste of money as the house was due to a much needed remodelling from top to bottom and some serious modernisation. I always knew this when I took the house on. I had hoped it wouldn't be for about five years. But in all fairness, I couldn't manage the gardening. It was too big and too crippling to my arthritis and for me financially it was out of my budget now. With no ability to earn at present it was a good time to re-evaluate.

My body can't manage the bending and digging. My poor back and legs retaliate when I try to crack on with minor gardening chores. Even minor weeding is a struggle just bending and fighting to get them out. They hang on for dear life. The little shits.

It's difficult for me and others to understand how much my illness has affected my body and how it manages my movements. It's a continuous learning curve. Understanding or not. I have to start to accept that I won't improve, rest is the key to gain small bits of a better quality of life.

My driven behaviour is a big no no…. in my future. My whole life has now to be micromanaged as they say. Any decisions I make, have to ensure I am doing for the right reason.

My options, again not too many.

That sounds really harsh. I really don't mean it to. I had initially explored living in a static caravan as it would suit my budget and needs. All on one level with no stairs and a small outside space. The only issue with that was the distance from my family and Kurt.

I know I do love and care for Kurt, very much. He is my soul mate and so easy to be with. My life would be empty without him. What I am questioning is my current ability to make the right decision. I don't want to hurt or offend anyone. Especially not Kurt when he has helped me so much since this crazy illness too hold again.

Kurt has looked after me and opened his home to me. Would I like to live with him? Yes, I would. We balance one another really well. He's clean, he cooks, rather well I must say. He shops, knows what he's doing and irons and washes. So very well house trained. So why be hesitant.

Well, we've both been on our own for a long time and that leads to us both having many bad habits and doing exactly what we want when we want. That can sometimes be a hard plaster to pull off. That said we both want someone to share life and holidays with. Which we have already

practiced playing house and experimented by going on a driving holiday together to the South of France, earlier in our relationship and greatly enjoyed. Both of us were surprised at how well we have both got on and how similar we are.

Taurus and stubborn Aries, we many need to use, I'll rephrase that, I need to use the verbal zip before I speak. Thinking before I open my mouth. Which when I'm well can tend to run away with itself. I can't say I have found Kurt guilty of that. Kurt is very laid back and calm.

I seem to have been able to curb my need to speak before thinking since my illness. I really haven't felt the need to communicate much at all. But as time goes on, I do feel myself getting back to my normal self and I know I need to think before I speak. I don't want to hurt Kurt for just being Kurt. Neither of us are prefect nor who's to say which one's way is right.

Ideally while writing, I am happier isolated which allows me to write at crazy impulsive times when my unpredictable brain allows me to. For example, I woke up at 5.00am this morning. My head full of ideas dropping into place. I can't wait to put pen to paper or fingers to typewriter. Not particularly a very sociable time while others are sleeping, but it is my brains time. It wants to write when it wants to write.

Sometimes it's exactly the opposite. I'll start to write late after a sleepy or dark day and when my brain finally feels better, I will carry on late into the night up to four am. My brain really is unpredictable. I'm sure there are other writers out there who have experienced the same.

Victor Hugo would remove his clothes and give them to his servant. I don't propose to go that far but from reading about other writers' idiosyncrasies and there are many, I am not on my own. Years ago writers used to meet in Parisienne Cafes and drink the odd bottle of Absinthe which was very popular at the time. Mine stimuli are more like a delayed switch that only comes on when its ready to be creative. Once that happens my gratitude to have my brain back is so great that no matter what time it is. I go and get coffee or a beer, dependant on what time it is, and light a cigarette. The words come to my fingertips like verbal diarrhoea.

I am so surprised as to where they have all come from. I write without thought, to capture everything before my brains had enough. Mostly this urge can go on for hours. Many hours where I am in oblivion of time. My excitement at being able to come up with so much amazes me.

Everything seems to fall into place like a domino effect, once I start to write all the thoughts and ideas of the past and present that were previously not forthcoming flow so fast. It's a good job they're not a river otherwise I'd be knee deep in water. The water would be coming down the hill so fast I wouldn't be able to keep up with it.

Once I am spent. It's like having a really good shag. My mind and body are totally fulfilled and exhausted. Every little note; slip of paper, idea, all in its perfect place. I marvel at my ability to put all the parts of the jigsaw together so smoothly. It's like watching an amazing firework display. Every firework plays its part exactly in tune to the music. I hope and pray that every time I sit down and write, no matter what time of day or night it is, that it brings me this complete fulfilment.

While laying cuddly and warm in Kurt's bed my brain keeps saying, come on get up. Writing isn't something I can control. I try to nap and snuggle ever closer to Kurt, but my random brain keeps niggling me. Prodding me and waking me from my lovely naps and cuddles of the big soft

man at my side. Finally, I have to get up. Guilt ridden, I am relaxing and wasting time. The words and ideas come at such strange times.

Our home is full of bits of papers and notebooks everywhere. Writing is managing me. Which in one way is wonderful in another I feel like I've lost control.

Having been a control freak for the last forty plus years I don't think that is a bad thing.

What is good, is that I understand that my brain can't remember every good idea I have and when I try to recall the idea, I have forgotten the important details.

Hence my library shelf of over twenty travel notebooks and the endless, post its I have around to jot ideas on as and when they come into my brain. They are a God send. I just gather the, post it's up and either type them into the current writing project I'm working on or put them into my notebooks under headings. I use a similar process when I'm traveling on trains and busses.

Although, I must say that often the writing takes some translating. Every time the driver takes a bump or curbs the pavement…bump bump and drops down the other side, my pen dances in the opposite direction I want it too. The writing resembles that of a pre schoolchild. Still workarounds are a life saver for my forgetful brain. Once so sharp, now needing endless work arounds to help me get the same result. But I'm happy to have found them and they work for me. It's great to have a success under my belt. However small. When days have so many whoopsies in them. I am thankful for small mercies.

Chapter 24

103 deaths were reported in the UK
up to the 16th March 2020 from Corona V

All Change the start of a very different time to come.

4.00am 12th March 2020 at Kurt's,

I woke up with a start. After an unbelievably bad night tossing and turning finally having enough and I got up at four for a cigarette and some water. I try to switch the television on to catch up on the corona virus news from China and Italy. The television yelled at me on top note. I switched it off straight away. I had no patience for messing with the two gadgets which balanced the Television and its many stations.

To be fair, Kurt has more TV technology than I had at my house. If I'd paid attention when he was very kindly showing me how it all worked, made notes even, I might have been wiser. Unfortunately, I was having a bad day when he was explaining the TV's many functions. So, I only had myself to blame for the loud noise I'd just made waking half the block up at 4.00am.

Fortunately, I have my phone set up for news updates on daily Corona V figures in the UK so, that would do. My patience was zero. I was tired and fed up. I went back to bed at six to try and again a few hours' sleep before my return journey home. I really wanted to get some good rest.

That was all I focused on when I crept into bed and put my arms around Kurt to warm up. I must have gone out like a light.

When I woke up at nine thirty. I was shocked that I had slept so long. I hadn't heard Kurt even go to work. I had sixty minutes to shower and get to the bus stop to get the bus to get me to my first appointment of the day in Chesterfield. It would be tight as I was still half asleep. But I knew I could make it.

The canal and the streets in Retford were deserted as I made my way to the bus stop. A few people were purposefully walking while ensuring they were keeping the required safe distance as was required of the new virus advice. We weren't yet on lock down, but everyone felt it was coming.

The hospital I had my appointment in was like a morgue. Not one soul had turned up for their appointment. I was straight in an out after having my boobs squashed into the appropriate machine. The nurses said it was either the lovely weather that had put people off or the Corona Virus advice.

They weren't sure which as no one had rung in to cancel.

Don't you just love how people waste NHS resources. No respect for the nurses at all. They take it all for granted. It's interesting to see how over the next two months attitudes change towards these valuable members of society.

Friday March 13th 2020.

I had been really looking forward to a girl's night out before I left Chesterfield to go and live at Kurt's. Tomorrow evening was our chosen evening for mayhem. Many bottles of chilled Prosecco and a fish and chip supper was out itinerary for the evening. This usually ended up being a messy evening. Either someone staggering in the middle of the road home or impatience waiting for a taxi. I wasn't sure how I'd cope with it as I hadn't been very sociable for a while, but I really wanted to do something before I started packing to move to Kurt's. I had picked the end of the month as my moving date as I wanted to be in Kurt's for my birthday on the 6th of April. A new beginning.

Little did I know how all the Corona Virus warnings of its spreading would affect us all. As the numbers started to rise in the UK and the warnings were becoming serious, not many of the girls were eager to attend in crowded pubs. Karen and I decided it would be the last time I would have the opportunity to see her for a while so we braved advice and really did enjoyed the beautiful sunny afternoon.

It was sadly the last time I would get to go to the pub for many months. The whole of Brampton must have felt the same way as it got really busy particularly, after seven O'clock. Every pub and its over spill on to the street was really buzzing. The atmosphere was like a bank holiday evening.

Karen and I, as hardened Brampton girls of old, who often enjoyed drinking along the Brampton mile, during our thirty year plus friendship, decided to start at a very civilised 2.00pm as was out tradition.

John Lowe, Karen's husband picked us up and we had our first couple of drinks with him. Which made it that I could catch up with him as well. (He didn't get asked to our girl's nights out. Strictly Girls only!) We then marched on further afield. Most places were quiet, so we were able to reminisce over the last thirty years of our lives. For a while there I thought I was a normal person. We had a great catch up and finished off with our traditional Fish & Chip supper and

then said out goodbyes. It was the last time I would hug my dear friend or any friend or family member for a good few month.

While on our evening out, we didn't hear the news that evening, the 13th March 2020, advice had become much stricter. Pubs were being advised to shut with immediate effect. Which as I am aware not everyone really took heed of that advice. The drinkers who were out, stayed out and continued to enjoy their evening as did we.

Friends who hadn't come to meet us were texting us to say we needed to come home as the police were going to visit pubs to make sure they were shutting. Well I have to say, we didn't see

any of that. The fish shop owner did say they would be shut after this evening. But life carried on until the close of business.

I guess this was the day that most people caught the first wave of Corona V. (as I had now Christened it. Later to be christened Corvid 19 by the Officials) Many people still mixed on that day and evening as self-isolation had not yet begun nor had the message really sunk in of the consequences even though China had just been through it.

The following day the start of panic buying by those who were really only thinking of themselves and toilet rolls were the first supply to run dry. People were buying them and stock piling. Entrepreneurs were selling them at up to £26 a roll on Face book. The madness had begun. I called these the Corona V Bog Roll Bandits. They had really shown their true colours. Fortunately, those who police face book put a stop to them their accounts were suspended.

My Doctor C. assessment which I had been waiting for so long was changed to a telephone assessment. After missing one another several times. (As I'm inclined to put my phone on silent, I didn't see the light flash to tell me there was an unidentified caller. When I realised that I had missed three calls as there was no name attached to her number my phone wouldn't put the call through. I'd obviously been fiddling with it and disabled something)

Panic set in. I really didn't want to miss this call. I finally manged to ring her and had someone to talk to who understood my psychological and physical issues and the reasons they had presented themselves so manifestly. Dr C. was amazing. She was astounded that I had never been offered trauma therapy before given all that I had been through over the last fifty years in my life.

We agreed that Dr C. would send me a copy of her report to further my needs for trauma therapy, which was being sent to The Health Psychology Service for advice as to whether I could benefit from EMDR (Eye movement desensitization and reprocessing) Or CFT (Compassion focused therapy) to see how I might benefit from their input. Dr C. did advise that the waiting list was long and could be anything from six months to a year before I heard from any department to take me to the next stage. She also cautioned that with the Corona V presenting itself more now that there could be a further delay.

Given how I was having so many ups and downs as was our world at this present time. I think this is where I finally decided I would need to try and see what self-intervention I could learn to help myself. I wasn't sure at this time how difficult or detrimental this would be, but something was surely better than all this nothingness.

Chapter 25

Corona V is here!
144 Deaths were announced in hospitals in the UK

19th March 2020

My second really bad night in a row. I'm really struggling to sleep well at present. Feel ratty. The past doesn't seem to want to stay buried. Fragments keep popping up in my dreams.

Something is really disturbing me. Having been through Corona V with Sophie and Peter, my brother and sister in law in China over the past two months on We Chat. I never expected it to reach the UK in such numbers.

Peter and Sophie were lucky they were on holiday in Kuala Lumpur when the outbreak hit China. Funnily It was at the time that I still couldn't shake my terrible flu and was struggling to breath and they were really worried about my lack of recovery.

We communicated every day and I kept them abreast of what was happening in China and elsewhere from our TV set. They didn't return to Beijing until the 19th of February as they weren't allowed back and had to go via Thailand where they self-isolated on one of the beautiful islands. I can't think of a lovelier place to rest. Once they were let back into Beijing, they had to self-isolate for another two weeks at Sophies mothers house and have been there ever since as the university in Baoding is only allowing online studies. All the students are now being taught online and will continue to be until September to ensure everyone's safety. I now see Prof P as I call my brother as a cartoon character in China teaching his students from his virtual classroom.

366 people died have in the UK
24th March 2020

I woke up this morning so restless. It was unreal. I finally realise what has been torturing my subconscious mind. I'm totally freaked out by the Corona V. I want to go out there and help but know I can't. I want to go out and help others ease their burden. My brain is so frustrated with my current condition.

My stiff back and feet that unexpectedly give up underneath me. The pain and speed at which I can move is slow and unpredictable. I never know when my right and left ankle now will decide to just jerk, and the nervous sharp pains cause me to lose my balance. The shooting pain is both unstable and mentally unbalancing my whole body and mind. I'm scared! I panic, I feel extremely vulnerable and incompetent. Completely insecure.

I want to get up and go out and help people. But I'm so scared of people and what they could give me. I feel guilty that I went out on March the 13th luckily 10 days on I feel fine.

I am trying to pack for my move the house is nearly done. I am selling the things that I won't need at Kurt's. Truthfully, I feel like I'm running away to a safe place. It's so far to the shops from my house. Essential times that we are allowed to shop for now I call emergency items. I don't go for milk. I'll drink my coffee black. I don't go for wine I'll drink water. I'll go to post a parcel for one of my jewellery customers or if I'm out of cigarettes. Sad but everyone's definition of essential varies.

425 died in the UK
Prince Charles has Corona V
25th March 2020 9.00am

The Corona V figures are still rising. For anyone who has not heard of Corona V I have a new friend. For those of you reading that don't know the facts about the coronavirus (Covid-19) or Corona V as I call it here are a few facts.

The virus has spread to nearly every country in the world. It is said that it first emerged in China at the beginning of the year. Some of us in the UK and around the world had a really bad flu with a four to six week barking cough and struggled to breath in November 2019 with remarkably similar symptoms. A lot of us didn't finally recover from it until the end of February.

More than 5.6 million people who have been tested have been infected there could be many more, but we have not tested everyone in the world yet. Around the world 351,000 people have died that we know of. Different countries have varying ways to count the death tolls. Up to the 27th May 2020, 37,460 have died from the virus in the UK.

Coronaviruses are a family of viruses that cause disease in animals. Only seven, including the Corona V, have made the jump to humans, as far as we know. We still have a lot to learn about it. Most Coronaviruses have symptoms the same as what we know as flu in humans.

It's said that Covid-19 is closely related to severe acute respiratory syndrome (SARS) which infected around 8,000 people and killed about 800 in 2003 to 2004. People who contracted SARS were seriously ill which made it easier to control and eradicate.

Since 2012 a Middle East respiratory syndrome (MERS-CoV), another of the family of coronavirus has been rearing its ugly head irregularly with 2,500 cases and under 900 deaths. Its infected Camels, bats and humans. Most of the cases are found in the Arabian Peninsula and those associated with travel to or from that area. There is currently no vaccine for MERS.

It's said that Corona V is different to the above two, as the scale of the disease is wide-ranging, causing 80 per cent of its cases to lead to only a mild infection. It is also said that many people could be carriers without displaying any symptoms.

So truthfully, it's a slippery little sucker and we really need to be aware as the government keeps telling us. We have a lot to learn about it.

I know one thing for sure. If you suffer from anxiety and depression it really takes you to another level of angst. As well as seeing everyone as a threat on my bad days I also see everyone as a carrier if they try and invade my personal space as it's a fact that someone can breathe it onto you. Urgh... and that scares the shit out of me.

Why, well most people are lovely and care about others but unfortunately our society today has a small account of angry, ignorant, selfish people who think its funny to abuse rules and don't care if they infect someone.

In my teenage years people got VD or Aids and anyone who contracted either were supposed to contact their partners to advise them they had it, to stop the spread and abstain from sexual relations with other partners. Did they no! What happened it spread. It took a lot longer to get under control because people will be people for their own reasons. Usually selfish ones. Hopefully, this time people will learn. We don't care how you got it. Get treated. Save lives.

Chapter 27

Kindness is free
468 died in the UK

My Little bird. – Insert from my today's Facebook message.
26th March 2020

Not something I go overboard with. I like to be a private person. But sometimes you see something that really touches you and it is worth sharing………

"I have a new friend. Thankfully for Kurt's creation to fed him through the winter. He comes every day." A little hungry bird.

"Yesterday I thanked a lady in the supermarket for coming to work and enabling me to buy food and cigarettes.

Up until this moment I felt totally helpless in giving anything back to society. Given my resent worsening of my mental and physical disabilities. My personal need to get up and volunteer to share my many skills are not wasted at home writing this.

I know now that even the little things count. The lady that served me at Retford, Asda was so nervous serving me she was nearly in tears. She was so thankful for my appreciation of her as she said everyone else just gave her abuse.

How bloody selfish can society be. Don't abuse the people that enable us to buy necessities. Or the people who go to the hospitals to save us.

"Would you stand in a shop for 8 hours serving people who could be spreading the virus unknowingly?"

"Like the little bird visitor, who rewards me when he is tweeting his songs and breaks my loneliness, one small word of thanks or kind deed is all it takes. It's free and it's human.

If you can't help people feel better don't be the coward that abuses them.

A grateful person to all who are helping us. I am only sorry I'm not standing there with you. Big Hug and love to all. Be safe. Vx"

The lovely lady, I referred to, serves me every time I go into shop there. She's so customer friendly along with her friend who works on the counter with her. Unfortunately, I don't know their names otherwise I would name them. To be honest all the staff in the little Asda are lovely and welcoming. Everyone, one of them. They all have time to help you when you're looking for something.

No one deserves the back of someone's nasty tongue just because the marketplace can't supply what it did last week, or items are rationed so that other people can buy them as well.

Given, that someone else's greed has created the situation by stock piling. Let's be reasonable about sharing a piece of the cake with everyone. Let's stop the selfishness. It's really not necessary.

I have to hobble to the supermarket to combine my exercise with shopping. You don't see me complaining. I'm happy to get out and see some smiling faces. I'm grateful my leg holds up to let me go. Granted Kurt does most of our shopping. So, mine is more of a mooch. I am one of the lucky ones. Before I moved here shopping was my hell! Wondering where things were and how would I carry things home or to the bus.

When you don't go far, the last thing you want to see is people nearly in tears because someone has shouted at them because someone's favourite item is out of stock. Seriously, how sad is that. Bulling and blaming a shop assistant who gets paid peanuts.

You know what? That is someone else's favourite item too. So bloody well get over it and eat something else or try a different brand. Don't take it out on the staff. It's their job to take your money not your abuse. Ars..hole! So, leave them alone! Go and abuse your car instead see how that feels. The rest of us love them and are really grateful their keeping the world of food moving for us. (That's the end of my rant to the ungrateful people in this world) One word! Respect !!

Now I need a nap. I've exhausted myself just writing about this.

But not before I listen to 'We are the World', to remind me of the wonderful people out there who want to work together, sing together, and share the world together. It brings positivity back to me and wipes out the darken thoughts that negative people bring to my brain

Chapter 28

578 deaths in the UK.
(from 17.00pm 26th March 2020 reported today)

That's scary! The slippery sucker is getting more of us.
Corona v or not?
27th March 2020

At 6.00am, I wake up, so early. I'm feeling desperate I need to hear the latest news. The Corona V situation is getting even more scary daily. People are dropping like flies. Every day the figure gets larger and we haven't hit the peak yet. Todays, local confirmed cases in Kurt's area of the country, Nottingham are 109 and in mine, Derbyshire 139.

I was going back to my house to finish packing this afternoon. But given that Kurt lives in Nottinghamshire I am thinking we are safer here. Even though I know that it will just be us two finishing off the packing at my house for my move to Kurt's. I am still feeling nervous about going to the doctors to pick up my last prescription before I move over here permanently.

I know it's irrational, but my fears just mount daily.

The last two times I went to the doctors I had my temperature taken before I was allowed in. Not a problem. I just feel guilty or even scared if I'm honest. I don't want to get a similar flu or whatever it was last time. I've only just started to feel better.

Yesterday I was engulfed by sleep. Again, the Darkness starting creeping in. I think there's too much information around. I am my own worst enemy. As I research to make sure my facts are correct for this book the worse, I feel. There is so much information out there in the media I just exhaust myself totally. There is so much conflicting information or maybe it is my disturbed brain struggling to fathom out the correct order of the figures. When reports say, at five pm on

the day before the death toll is Xxxx. It means, not today's death toll, as it states, but the day before. Nothing is simple.

My eyes protest and want to close. That in itself really drives me nuts. I feel the need to know and understand who my illness is affecting by this Pandemic. Yet my mind won't let me do it to its best. Bloody infuriating.

"Kick into gear brain and work like you used to please!"

Yesterday I read about the first British man to contract Covid-19 (Corona v as I call it). A Welsh teacher Connor Read age 25 who was teaching English in Wuhan. As Connor detains his experience, I can't help but still feel how similar his condition was to what I had in November in the UK. It's too close for comfort. And yet he was all those miles away. Conner describes what it's really like to catch the coronavirus. He describes it as the worst disease he has ever had. It left him sweating, shivering, and struggling to breathe as his eyes burned and bones ached.

In November, he became the first British man to catch the deadly Corona V or did he?

I'm not big on conspiracy theories and God knows Facebook and the internet is full of interesting, fantastic, versions from people everywhere theorising about the contraction of the virus and how it first started and where. All of them ranging from Wuhan market to foreign powers man made chemical weapons. The list is endless. I won't bore you with it!

What I do know is that one day the truth will come out. All the speculation will be put to bed, and our great scientists and researchers will get to the bottom of it. A cure will be found and life,

I won't say will go back to normal. That would be unrealistic. I would say people in our world will learn from it and make the world a kinder safer place to be. Our attitudes towards one another will be more loving and respectful for all the pieces of life's jigsaw we represent and realise how much we need each other.

Not wishing to be one of the Corona V, people but the possibility could now be getting closer to a reality. I too had something my son and family somehow gave me, which I thought was flu.

In November, while Che was visiting me to drop the kids off for a half term visit of four days, we think that we shared more thank memories and Nannies favourite carrots. It's the only time I've been that close to anyone and done lots of kissing and cuddling with the kids. I hadn't seen them for a few weeks, so we had lots of catching up to do.

It rained all through their visit, so we spent most of our time indoors. Cuddling up on the sofa and watching movies at night. Spookily. No one only Kurt normally gets that close to me.

My eldest Granddaughter Chloe was really run down and poorly taking some antibiotics. She had been to the doctors before she came. But not really diagnosed with anything other than the usual virus we all get at this time of the year. Particularly when it's so damp. She was struggling to eat normally and had a sore throat and generally felt crap. She wanted more cuddles than normal for a fifteen-year-old. So, we watched a couple of late night films together and rebounded. We'd missed one another a lot.

When Chloe was younger, she had slept at my house every weekend from being a baby. As she grew up, we did lots of wonderful things together and got really close. As time has gone on and she has grown up and I have moved a lot with work there haven't been so many   opportunities. So, it was great to spend some quality time together.

Our re bonding was wonderful. Cuddles always seem to make the world feel better.

Below is how Conner Read, explains how he beat the Corona V illness that is sweeping across the globe and causing us all so much disruption and grief.

He explains his Corona V symptoms, what they are and when you should seek the help of a doctor?

(By Connor or The Daily Mail Published: 22:08, 4 March 2020 | Updated: 19:07, 5 March 2020) An extract.

In Connors own words below his diarised version of his illness has me feeling like I'm starring in the mirror. It's so Déjà vu. It would be interesting to see how many other people felt this way in November, December of 2019 and feel the same when they read his words below.

I've certainly spoken to a few people who felt the same and struggled for the same length of time with the same symptoms and went through the same hell.

These were all people who knew something was wrong and different from the flu they normally get around this time of the year but weren't sure exactly what it is. There are so many different viruses in the world these days. It's become difficult to know when to go to the doctors, you feel like you're being a nuisance and other people are worse off then you. You hope it will shake itself off. There was no shaking this off anywhere.

Connor Reed, a 25-year-old expat teacher from Llandudno in North Wales, was the first British man, who taught in Wuhan to catch the Corona V. From coughs and aches to burning up and spending the night in hospital, here's how he beat the illness that is sweeping the globe.

Day 1: Monday November 25: I have a cold. I'm sneezing and my eyes are a bit bleary. It isn't bad enough to keep me off work. I arrived in this country to teach English as a foreign language — but now I'm a manager at a school in Wuhan, the city in central China where I have lived for the past seven months.

I speak Mandarin well, and the job is interesting. My cold shouldn't be very contagious, so I have no qualms about going to work. And I live alone, so I'm not likely to give it to anyone. There hasn't been anything in the news here about viruses. I have no cause for concern. It's just a sniffle.

Day 2: I have a sore throat. Remembering what my mum used to do when I was a child, I mix myself a mug of honey in hot water. It does the trick.

Day 3: I don't smoke, and I hardly ever drink. But it's important to me to get over this cold quickly, so that I can stay healthy for work. For medicinal

175

purposes only, I put a splash of whisky in my honey drink. I think it's called a 'hot toddy'.

Day 4: I slept like a baby last night. Chinese whisky is evidently a cure for all known ailments. I have another hot toddy in the evening.

Day 5: I'm over my cold. It really wasn't anything.

Day 7: I spoke too soon. I feel dreadful. This is no longer just a cold. I ache all over, my head is thumping, my eyes are burning, my throat is constricted. The cold has travelled down to my chest and I have a hacking cough. This is flu, and it's going to take more than a mug of honey with or without the magic whisky ingredient.

The symptoms hit me this afternoon like a train and, unless there's an overnight miracle, I will not be going to work tomorrow. It's not just that I feel so ill — I really don't want to give this flu to any of my colleagues.

Day 8: I won't be in work today. I've warned them I'll probably be off all week. Even my bones are aching. It's hard to imagine I'm going to get over this soon.

Even getting out of bed hurts. I am propped up on pillows, watching TV and trying not to cough too much because it is painful.

Day 9: Even the kitten hanging around my apartment seems to be feeling under the weather. It isn't its usual lively self, and when I put down food it doesn't want to eat. I don't blame it – I've lost my appetite too.

Day 10: I'm still running a temperature. I've finished the quarter-bottle of whisky, and I don't feel well enough to go out and get any more. It doesn't matter I don't think hot toddies were making much difference.

Day 11: Suddenly, I'm feeling better, physically at least. The flu has lifted. But the poor kitten has died. I don't know whether it had what I've got, or whether cats can even get human flu. I feel miserable.

Day 12: I've had a relapse. Just as I thought the flu was getting better, it has come back with a vengeance. My breathing is laboured. Just getting up and going to the bathroom leaves me panting and exhausted. I'm sweating, burning up, dizzy and shivering. The television is on, but I can't make sense of it.

By the afternoon, I feel like I am suffocating. I have never been this ill in my life. I can't take more than sips of air and, when I breathe out, my lungs sound like a paper bag being crumpled up. This isn't right. I need to see a doctor. But if I call the emergency services, I'll have to pay for the ambulance call-out myself. That's going to cost a fortune. I'm ill, but I don't think I'm dying — am I?

Surely, I can survive a taxi journey. I decide to go to Zhongnan University Hospital because there are plenty of foreign doctors there, studying. It isn't rational but, in my feverish state, I want to see a British doctor. My Mandarin is pretty good, so I have no language problem when I call the taxi. It's a 20-minute ride. As soon as I get there, a doctor diagnoses pneumonia. So that's why my lungs are making that noise. I am sent for a battery of tests lasting six hours.

Day 13: I arrived back at my apartment late yesterday evening. The doctor prescribed antibiotics for the pneumonia but I'm reluctant to take them — I'm worried that my body will become resistant to the drugs and, if I ever get really ill and need them, they won't work. I prefer to beat this with traditional remedies if I can.

It helps, simply knowing that this is pneumonia. I'm only 25 and generally healthy: I tell myself there's no reason for alarm. I have some Tiger Balm. It's like Vick's vapour rub on steroids. I pour some into a bowl of hot water and sit with a towel over my head, inhaling the fumes. And I've still got the antibiotics in reserve if I need them.

Suddenly, I'm feeling better, physically at least. The flu has lifted.

Day 14: Boil a kettle. Add Tiger Balm. Towel over head. Breathe for an hour. Repeat.

Day 15: All the days are now blurring into one.

Day 16: I phone my mother in Australia. There was no point in calling her before now — she'd only worry and try to jump on a plane. That wouldn't work it takes an age to get a visitor's visa to China. I'm glad to hear her voice, even if I can't do much more than croak, 'Mum, I feel so ill.'

Day 17: I am feeling slightly better, but I don't want to get my hopes up yet. I've been here before.

Day 18: My lungs no longer sound like bundles of broken twigs.

Day 19: I am well enough to stagger out of doors to get more Tiger Balm. My nose has cleared enough to smell what my neighbours are cooking, and I think I might have an appetite for the first time in nearly two weeks.

Day 22: I was hoping to be back at work today but no such luck. The pneumonia has gone — but now I ache as if I've been run over by a steamroller. My sinuses are agony, and my eardrums feel ready to pop. I know I shouldn't but I'm massaging my inner ear with cotton buds, trying to take the pain away.

Day 24: Hallelujah! I think I'm better. Who knew flu could be as horrible as that?

Day 36: A tip-off from a friend sends me hurrying to the shops. Apparently, the Chinese officials are concerned about a new virus that is taking hold in the city. There are rumours about a curfew or travel restrictions. I know what this will mean — panic buying in the shops. I need to stock up on essentials before everyone else does.

Day 37: The rumours were right. Everyone is being told to stay indoors. From what I've heard, the virus is like a nasty dose of flu that can cause pneumonia. Well, that sounds familiar.

Day 52: A notification from the hospital informs me that I was infected with the Wuhan coronavirus. I suppose I should be pleased that I can't catch it again — I'm immune now.

179

However, I must still wear my face mask like everyone else if I leave the apartment, or risk arrest. The Chinese authorities are being very thorough about trying to contain the virus.

Day 67: The whole world has now heard about coronavirus. I've told a few friends about it, via Facebook, and somehow the news got out to the media.

(Women wear masks as they shop in London, Britain today. Since the outbreak became international news, I've seen hysterical reports (especially in the U.S. media) that exotic meats such as bat and even koala are on sale at the fish market. I have never seen that)

My local paper back in Llandudno, North Wales, has been in touch with me. Maybe I caught the coronavirus at the fish market.

It's a great place to get food on a budget, a part of the real Wuhan that ordinary Chinese people use every day, and I regularly do my shopping there.

The only slightly weird sight I've seen is the whole pig and lamb carcasses for sale, with their heads on.

Day 72: Tuesday, February 4: It seems the newspapers think it's terrific that I tried to cure myself with hot toddies.

I attempt to explain that I had no idea at the time what was wrong with me — but that isn't what they want to hear.

The headline in the New York Post says, 'UK teacher claims he beat coronavirus with hot whisky and honey.'

I wish it had been that easy.

Connor Read.

I really can't thank Connor enough. Poor Connor I really feel like I've been on the same journey. Sometimes when your mentally ill you think you are over exaggerating the situation because of your anxieties. But as you've read above my November was a similar experience last year. Then I felt better in December and went to Germany. Totally unaware barking my head off around the Christmas Markets and in Hotel bedrooms propped up on pillows. Sweating and shaking. Jesus, I feel so guilty.

That said, I did go to the doctors before I went to Germany and was sent to the Nurse. But as my temperature had gone down and she thought I was on the road to recovery. I was dismissed as having flu telling me to go home and do all the things I had been doing before. Paracetamols, Vick rub etcetera. No tests no antibiotics. The nurse did ask me if I smoked and when I told her I had the odd few the appointment was over very quickly.

I started to feel better so I thought the fresh air in the Black forest in Germany would do me good.

We stocked up with meds and sucking tables and off we went.

We were driving so I really didn't give it second thought. I was hoping the happiness of doing Christmassy things would help lift my already heavy depression along with the fresh mountain air would heal and refresh my lungs.

One evening, I got so wet, while walking round the market in Schwäbische Halle. There were so many people out enjoying the beautiful picturesque ancient market with its many attractions there was little shelter from the minute droplets of sticky rain. It was the sort of little rain that settled on you. Exceptionally fine, annoying and soaked you through to the skin.

We persevered to get some food as we'd been looking forward to it all day. Wonderful barbequed steaks cooked in front of us. So tasty, washed down with a special Glühwein with rum. That was a first for me and I hadn't tasted that before. (Surprising having lived there for seven years) It really hit the spot, with the brass band playing from the little covered stage on the square and people singing it was only the maddening drizzle which ruined it. Then the drizzle turned to snow, and the scene was idyllic. Expect for my constant coughing. My dry chocking coughs and gasping for breath.

I was barking so loud at one stage that when I passed the Pharmacy, I made myself go in. I didn't want another sleepless night of coughing and being propped up on pillows all night. I popped in to see if they had any magic remedies for me. The pharmacist advised some vitamin C sucking sweets which had some medicine in them would go straight to the sore throat which would ease the choking and soreness because of all the coughing. I bought two packets and couldn't wait to open them and see if they worked.

The pharmacist did mention that she had been prescribing this to many people as there was a lot of this type of coughing around.

We had one more market to visit and an overnight stay in Rothenberg, a beautiful Old town with a medieval Christmas market which was famous for its Christmas decorations. People travel to see it from all over the world. I wanted to show it to Kurt along with the amazing old town and its fortifications. I'd booked us a hotel right in the old Town, so I didn't have too far to walk with parking. I was desperate for a good night's sleep and to enjoy my last couple of days.

I had planned this holiday with Kurt since our summer holiday in the South of France in July. Every place I had researched for its uniqueness as every market was different. And all I've done is gone through them all and cough and bark like an old dog. Lord please give me a few days peace and enjoyment to relive this beautiful place my Tanta Christel used to bring me to and let me share my memories with Kurt.

The sucking pastels gave me extraordinarily little relief. I was so disappointed. I was in a lot of pain and barked for most of the night. There was no comfortable position to be found in or on my beautiful bedroom.

When we got up and drew the curtains the next morning everywhere was covered in snow. It looked so magic. The Cathedral steps, the Christmas trees all lit up and the beautiful market stalls with their unique goods. After a leisurely breakfast we packed and set off in the snow to Rothenburg ob. der Tauber, known for its medieval architecture, I was so excited.

The cough seemed to abate while I was sat up. Once I tried to lay down or something irritated my throat the whole painful barking, the headache and dizziness returned. It was the cruellest flu I had ever know. Half my time in Rothenberg was spent eating pea soup and lying in bed coughing. Such a beautiful place, such a shame. On our sea crossing I stayed in bed I felt so rough.

When we returned from Germany on the December 16th, I went straight home to self-isolate myself because I didn't want to be in contact with Kurt as he seemed to have got over his much milder cold??

I went to my house in Chesterfield to bed for seven days. Cuddled up in my beautiful duvet feeling sorry for myself I stayed there until I had the energy to get up and start eating again with my anti-depressants and paracetamols. I felt so miserable and wretched drinking only boiled water and eating the odd piece of toast. The barking did continue for some time and many pillows were required to sleep, to try and lessen the chocking. I hated it. I had never had anything so bad.

Once many years ago when I was over worked and run down, I got a real flu and that floored me, and I spend two weeks in bed unable to move. Full of aches and pains but never this relentless coughing. My memories of it were as clear as yesterday. It was real flu something I had never experienced before.

Colds were easy to deal with. I only ever caught those in summer. But this current episode I could only put down to my chemicals being so imbalanced and not being able to fight both the pains in my ankle and resist the virus. That on top of the anxiety and depression I was really turning out to be a crap date for Kurt.

Bless, he was so easy going and tolerant of everything. I couldn't have found a kinder loveable man. I love him and I wonder if he even knows it.

It was another two weeks after our return that I finally felt able to go out and all the dizziness subsided completely. The Children came to see me on Christmas Eve, and we had a family dinner. I had another bloody cold. Much milder thankfully and have only just shook the whole episode. Thankfully two weeks ago.

I've just heard on the news that Our Prime Minister Boris Johnson (55) has been tested positive with the Corona V so he will be governing from isolation. I hope he has a soft comfy feather duvet. I know why they called them comforters now. There is nothing like it. Warm cuddly and secure. It really is the only place to be when you feel so wretched.

I will never know if it was Corona V I had unless I get tested which is unlikely at present. And let's hope it never comes back again. I would not wish anything like that on my worst enemy. Cruel, vile, relentless, and so difficult to recover from. I know I'm getting older, but I wouldn't want a repeat performance of the last three months.

I have always refused the flu jab. Having heard so many horror stories about the lousy condition it puts you in I have fought against it venomously for years. You know, after what I've just been through, I wouldn't take much persuasion to have it next year. That for me is a real turnround. It will be a long time before I forget how bad this was.

My greatest concern now is, am I a carrier. How will I ever know.

News flash, today the Lake District has shut down the first time ever. A place with so much fresh air, space and beauty. Nothing is exempt from this nasty vicious virus.

Chapter 29

How Corona V is affecting people with Mental Health issues.

at 17.00pm last night deaths in the UK reached 759

28th March 2020

07.30am. My crazy dreams startle me as I awaken, I reach for my phone, the deaths are rising fast now. It's scary. The rapid increase follows the same pattern as the other countries. The Corona V. is jumping higher and higher taking people in larger numbers now and will I fear for the next week or so.

My dreams are filled with angst. Jumbled and totally disorientated. Who's going to look after Oliver when we are all gone? He can't be left by himself. He needs us to survive. What if we all get wiped out and only Oliver is left. I know he is clever and resourceful but all I have left in my dream is my sweet darling grandson is standing there lost. I want to cuddle him but it's just a dream. I miss him so much. I awaken so startled the dream is so vivid. My heart is breaking for him. Why, are these bloody dreams tormenting me so much with this nonsense. I wish they'd piss off and give me some peace.

Now my emails are updating, the first one to greet me is doom, Apple News quoting an article in Esquire. This is how experts think Corona V will change the world over the next eighteen months. Seriously, let me wake up first before you terrorise me with your negative disaster stories. Let me at least take my tablets and breathe before I get the next dose of what sells papers.

Ok, so todays tale of woe is that whether the pandemic lasts two months or two years, the way we live, and work will change for ever. Really thank you for stating the obvious. Yes, we all

know we may need to consider don't things differently for a while until we get things under control. But why wake me up to all this doom and gloom. We'll work it out. I try to be positive. Even in my wonky state of mind. I have to be.

These news articles should be banished from telling their tales of woe. The truth is no one knows what's going to happen. Let's take it one day at a time. The government has tried to help as much as it can. We just need to keep our heads and work through it. Stick together help one another and we will prevail.

Instead of looking at it as the worse disaster ever. Yes, it's bad but we will get there!! It's called survival. Even in these black dark times. The article does on and on about isolation and self-distancing. Well let's look at self-distancing and someone who struggles with metal health issues prior to Corona V and now and how this is affecting them and me.

Things that Society has forgotten about people with mental illnesses. (or were never aware)

From my personal perspective and experience.

I already try to social distance myself, a lot. People just don't give me the space or understand in today's society.

"Ok so I don't have a badge on beware! Your invading my personal space!"

I go shopping when it's the quietest. Why? because, I don't want to bump into anyone and talk to them. I don't go with people who offer to help because my mind can't always cope with them.

I go when it's quiet because I'm disabled, and I don't want people staring at me when my foot goes or I'm limping so I go when I know no one else will be there. No kids to ask why I limp.

I go when there are the least people out because I don't want people tutting at me when I forget what I'm doing or I'm slow. So, ok it takes me one hour to walk round and buy a small trolley full. That small trolley lasts me a month, so I don't have to come back again. Even my friends don't get it. They rush around and are impatient with me. People don't get how difficult life is for me.

189

Disorientation isn't a nice place to be. It's bloody shit to be truthful.

I only go to the cigarette queue when the queue is short, so I don't become agitated with people for no reason. When the smallest thing agitates it takes me all myself control not to shout at shop assistants who are just sharing polite conversation instead of serving people. It scares me how angry I get for no reason. I have to talk myself into staying there or do without.

When there are more people in the shops there is a greater chance of bumping into aggressive humans. I've always been agitated by people arguing in shops. Washing their family's dirty knickers in public. Really!! I want to scream at them to stop. I don't want to hear their business. Or who's slept with whom. Sometimes even fighting. I've watched men throwing their fists in the air at women, drunk. Being so abusive it triggers my anxiety and I want to stop them. It's enough to put me off shopping for life.

When I'm standing at the bus station and someone accosts me to discuss his religious beliefs. That same person, then follows me onto a bus tries to sit next to me to continue in his loudest voice so everyone can hear him. With no thought of how that bothers me.   How anxious and angry he is making me. I try to smile and show understanding, but I just want to get off at the next stop for some peace. But he keeps inflicting his opinions on me and everyone on the bus. us all. He is not aware how he is intruding into my personal space and

190

affecting me. He only cares about the sound of his own voice. I want to run a mile to escape him. Really difficult on a bus.

When people start pushing in a queue, getting closer and closer to get on the bus coughing all over the place not caring who they breathe over. I want to give them a hankie to make them aware they are spreading germs. Spiting and it just misses my foot as if it's an everyday occurrence. What a bloody peasant! I really don't want to catch that bus anymore. I have to find a time when there are no people waiting there.

When I go for a walk along the canal at the back of Kurt's for a little fresh air. A mother passes with me with her five year old and starts f ..ing and jeffing at her and tells her she a cu…t . Threatens to through her into the canal if she doesn't stop annoying her. Annoying her? Her behaviour reminds me of my childhood hell. What a horrible mother! My, peace is shattered. I'm agitated, my foot goes, and all pleasure goes out of what should have been a quiet, flat, slow walk in the sunshine. She is oblivious of her actions and how they have affected me. Or how her behaviour would affect others.

When going to the doctor's surgery and people are all crammed together in the seats. I have to go to reception and tell them I need to go outside because I can't cope with being around all those people. They tell me to return within ten minutes or how ever late the doctors are running. If they aren't, I find a magazine to distract me. Groups of people just agitate me for no reason sometimes.

Sad, but no one knows. I often wonder how many other people are as uncomfortable as I am.

While waiting to be served in a shop and the assistants are busy telling their life story to a friend and holding everyone up just because they can. (I know we have to be respectful and pleasant to all) There are endless signs up reminding us to be patient.

There is patience and being openly rude to the customers. Where is the sign that says, "if our shop assistances are otherwise engaged in idle gossip? Please let us know."

They have no idea why some of us only go out to shop when its quiet. Or don't go back at all because of how they have been made to feel. In the hope that the next shop's assistant's behaviour will be more considerate and obliging.

People with Mental Health issues as well as people without, do have the right to some space. To feel safe and not threatened when someone walks too close to them in the street, they think they're going to be mugged. Just because the other person has no patience and is in a hurry, doesn't give them the right to push slower people out of the way.

Just because the person in front of you is dawdling or studying a label, we should consider that maybe there is a reason. They could, like me be struggling to walk any quicker, or need to read the food label to ensure they are able to eat it'd contents safely.

I constantly walk with fear and trepidation when I hear footsteps behind me. My mind manages to conjure up all sorts of frightening scenarios. Something only gained recently since my, foots ability to move quickly and my ability to protect myself has diminished. I look behind me and let people pass. I don't want people too close to me.

Their closeness puts me in a bad place mentally. I feel like I'm scared of my own shadow. Me, who used to be such a tough lady, scared of nothing. It's unthinkable. But it is my reality now.

I'm scared to go out with a walking stick which would help my foot. I don't want people to see how vulnerable I really am. That is the true reality of my life now.

How many more people out there suffer like I do? Since I've recognised my condition, I have identified many. ... and no, they don't wear a sign or necessarily are in a wheelchair or carry a stick. They are simply different, unique! Lovely people who deserve a bit of understanding. Please be kind to them.

Chapter 30

Peoples Beautiful words on Facebook give me inspiration!

29th March 2020 death toll 1,148 figures reported today from 17.00pm of the 27th March.

While the news of everyday life and the death tolls in our countries current state in the Corona V pandemic gets ever more grim and depressing, I am reading the most beautiful pieces on Face showing how much people care an realise that their lives must change.

After reading so many lovely words and giving them much though. I wanted today to change something or repay someone back for a kindness. I found I need to look no further than on my own doorstep. I could work on improving our new life together at home.

I realised today that Kurt was looking after me too well. He'd been cooking lovely meals and shopping for food for us for the last three days. He would cook while I nap, in the afternoon and then wake me up when tea was ready. It was such a lovely thing to do. I didn't want to take it for granted.

While I was suffering from massive anxiety & depression. Brought on by reading and researching too much into the Corona V. My greed for too much information was bombarding for my brain. Both confusing it and over burdening it with information it wasn't ready to process yet in such large quantities.

Yet, as my driven personality pushed me for more knowledge, I became carried away in the wave of knowledge I was learning. I forgot I was ill and not managing my brains capacity to process so much all at once.

That, along with recently moving into Kurt's flat. I was slowly rearranging my furniture to fit into and wasn't aware it was tiring me. I was enjoying it all too much. I had started to start singing while I was working. I felt as thou I'd finally found where I fitted in life.

Every afternoon at twoish I would go for a nap and Kurt would wake me up tell me my tea was ready at five or so. I'd wake up in a start from a very deep satisfying sleep. Unaware of how long I had been there. This had gone on for three whole days now. At the same times. I would feel overwhelmed and slink off to bed and totally crash.

Today, I decided life would be different. I would need to work on how I can manage my time and energy levels so that I could cook Kurt a lovely meal in return for his kindnesses. That was my challenge. I needed to find a balance in my life. Not carry on the road back to total destruction and zombie land again. How many warnings did I need?

I set about planning how I could achieve this. Not too much research too early in the morning.

That was OK when I lived alone. There was no one else there to consider. I could sleep and eat whenever I wanted and write into the early hours of the next day. Then collapse with exhaustion.

All my energy was being channelled into my writing because I was so grateful that my ability to do it had been returned to me. With no thought of, food sleep, drink cleaning and washing.

I could live in the same PJ's for a couple of days until I was totally exhausted and knew that without food my brain would switch of again.

Funny how a body finds a different way of conveying messages to you when you won't listen.

It's like switching a light bulb off. Once it's off its dark. That's it. Eat, sleep, take your tablets but stop what you're doing because you're not well!!

It was now time to learn to live with its messages. I wouldn't say I had cracked it because I keep slipping back into the old habits which had caused me problems over the years. Somehow, I had to learn to understand all the signs and more importantly obey them. Which was something I was having trouble with. I was so giddy when the words came to me of what I need to express next and share. Everything else came second.

I would need to prep food earlier and cook food in bits so that it would all come together at teatime. This would enable me to take breaks. A balance needed to be found. Not that Kurt minded one bit. He loved to cook and was exceptionally good at it.

His food was always very tasty and creative. But I wanted to do my bit. I wanted to be fare with him

I had become aware that if I wanted to give this relationship the best shot I could I needed to find balance. This couldn't be all about me and my needs. Even though they had taken second place for so long. It was about the two of us making it together. He had been so kind and understanding since I'd meet him watched me fall and now rise up again slightly. I owed him so much. I loved him so much. I needed to get this right for both of us and our future.

So, listening to my brain and body was to be the start and tea was served at six and he loved it! Fajitas and did he love them! Mm mm Yum Yum . He did!

Chapter 31

Seven day furlough with pay!
1,408 deaths reported today
from the same source as before.
30th March 2020

The rise in deaths is alarming. Kurt came home an hour early today from work . Apparently, he had been coughing too much at work. He didn't look particularly pleased. Seven days at home on paid leave is fine with me. At least he will be safe. So I became chief shopper.

As an essential worker he was one of the people who could go to work. His area of work was appropriately segregated to enable self-distancing and one shift time ended before the other came in to minimise all contact.

Anyone now who is at work with any symptoms of Corona V is sent home on full pay for seven days isolation. Kurt's cough was nothing, but his work mates were concerned. The advice from the government is clear. A anyone with a cough, fever or loss of smell or taste must stay at home for seven days. They are not allowed to mix or leave the house. It was the way everyone was thinking at present. I am so jumpy if someone comes near me and coughs, so I found it understandable that other feel that way.

People were being advised to stay safe. Self-distancing of two meters apart from anyone they don't live with. Work from home if you can. Travel to work in your own car. Only one person

per household to go shopping and then follow the market out rules. Only essential workers to travel on public transport. No public gatherings of more than two people.

Luckily, most people seen to be following advice as the death rate keeps growing. Nothing will change within our new society until the death rate plateaus. Change will come when it's time for change to come. It's just going to be a long nerve racking time for all of us.

Friday March 13th 2020.

Figures expected to increase as previously only hospital deaths were counted. From today all nonhospital deaths will be added to the figure.

2nd April 2020

I've had a few really Dark days, can't seem to get myself to do anything. I really can't write when I'm so dark. Truthfully, I am crap at everything I try.

When I got for a short walk it's such an effort. The pain in the bottom of my back is torture. It's worse than having strong dragging period pains. It is so relentless with every step. Ruins every pleasure I have. Pain killers not working. I think I'd rather have period pains. At least with those you knew there was an end to them when time was up. This just comes back every morning the minute I get out of bed.

I'm walking like some sort of a wobble person. Yes, wobbling from side to side to try and balance both hip pains. Not a pleasant sight. I really wish they'd sort this shit out. It just makes my days darker. I try and start off positive then the pain stops everything going forward.

I do try and ignore it. But it's like a relentless child wanting something it can't have. It just keeps coming back for more again and again until I lay down flat. Hell, on earth.

I need to go to my house in Chesterfield to do the last clear out. Maybe my subconscious is stopping me. God knows I really don't get it. I wanted to be all moved for my birthday.

4th April 2020

Kurt and I finally set off go to Chesterfield for a couple of days to finish off the cleaning and bring the remainder of my possessions. I feel guilty that we are going because of the distance from Retford to Chesterfield we need to travel but as we won't be going near anyone and we are in the car it should be safe enough.

I'm concerned we are breaking government guidelines, on travelling out of our area, but I really can't afford the bills any longer or the unsettledness I feel at still having my things in two places. I long to get settled in one place. I feel like I've been a gypsy so long.

With Kurt helping it shouldn't take us too long to complete. I've done most of the cleaning and sorting on our trips at weekends to collect boxes over the last few weeks little by little. We are beginning to get overwhelmed with all the stuff at the flat. So much is hidden under the bed.

Just as I was worrying about where to put stuff next, Kurt came up with the idea of emptying the two cupboards in the hall and turning them into clothes and storage closets. Our only problem is that while we are in lock down, we can't have anyone round to do the woodwork required.

Patience is a real virtue at this time in our lives. Not something I have a massive amount of, but I am trying. Very trying! Kurt has an abundance of it for both of us thankfully. He's also been amazing at sharing and making space for me at his home to make my feel welcome and allowed me to put my stamp on places. I don't know if I'd have been so generous in my current state of mind. I learn a lot from him.

We don't manage to get everything in the car, so Kurt has offered to come back on Tuesday after work to get the remaining few things. I just can't cope with coming back.

My time at my house in Chesterfield has had so many highs and lows. I know I need to leave but I still have a feeling of unfinished business and failure. The friends I have come back to re kindle our relationships with, will feel let down. Even though I know that is only a distance issue.

The doctors in Chesterfield have helped me so much in a time of real time of crisis in my life. Friends have helped me to cope and encouraged me to stay. My garden has given me much outdoor pleasure and real thinking time.

The lack of my ability to find work to support this house has broken me totally. Both financially and mentally. It's initial feeling of a beautiful safe haven has turned into a massive financial burden. The joy and excitement that I got initially from having my garden things

around me and making the house my home has been destroyed by my bloody inability to have the energy or pain free ability to continue being creative here, have really taken its toll.

Having movement, bending, stretching, grasping and the energy to do things necessary to create the over ambitious vegetable garden have truly shown me exactly what I am not able to do.

Things, that once were such a pleasure are now just a constant worry. I pray for energy and the mental desire to keep it up will come. Unfortunately, neither the desire nor the energy returned to my body or mind. Every tiny weed I try to remove becomes more stubborn. Or was it my energy which was less. Whatever it is, it stopped me from producing the results of one small success.

This is the start of me admitting there are things I will never be able to achieve going forward. Bite size projects would only be achievable when my mind and body would allow. The approach to future projects would have to be the same as my current approach to ironing, cooking a meal, changing the bed and going to the shop.

I know this is sheer pants. But they say admission is the beginning of the road to recover. Some things are more difficult to admit to than others. But the journey has begun.

Chapter 32

A Birthday in Lock down.
6th April 2020

Celebrating my birthday in past years hasn't been a particularly great success. I have had good and bad ones. Given that my mother died the day before my eighteenth birthday, I've always been reluctant to celebrate. Her death still haunts me to this day. Having to grow up without a mother really did unleash my wildest side. (Well that's what I chose to call it)

That said, now the grandchildren, with Che and Kelly have always made my birthday a special occasion with lots of flowers, plants and wonderful cards filled in by the children and a surprise gift. This year a massive envelope was delivered to my door. I was intrigued at its size when the postman came to the door with it. The envelop was full of handwritten cards by my four grandchildren, one from my great grandchildren and of course Che and Kellies family.

It was simply wonderful to receive them all along with my Mother's Day cards which, I had missed because of the lock down. Little things please me. Simple thoughts that show people care. It was an absolutely wonderful display and brought a tear to my eye not being able to see their expectant little faces when I read them. Each card had its own special message either as a

204

message or by the handwriting in it. Bless them. I really do miss them all and our family get togethers.

Kurt and his sisters sent me some lovely cards too, a wonderful plant arrangement for my balcony and the promise of taking me shopping once this was all over. How wonderful even a lockdown birthday can be.

I mention to Kurt that I would be more than happy with a lovely rib eye steak for my birthday which he cooked to perfection. Polished off with my favourite Prosecco. What more could a girl want. Beautiful cards present, and food it felt like everyone one was there with me.

Chapter 33

Crazy Dreams and Not rights.

881 daily total deaths – still high and frightening.
9th April 2020

Since my birthday, my life has become dark. People are dying in far larger numbers daily now. Everyone scares me. I see them all as potential carriers. Even my dreams are being completely over the top.

All I can see is this turd the size of a Cumberland sausage. Its floating in the toilet basin. Struggling to fit in. Urgh, seriously who wakes up at 5.00am after such a dream. Where the hell did that come from? If, there is anyone out there who dissects dreams. Please feel free and write to me. Total madness??? We already know that one. A little more depth analysis required.

Who the bloody hell wakes up dreaming of something so bloody disgusting as that? The vision is so clear. I can't get it out of my mind. In my vision I am still starring at it wondering how on earth it's going to flush down the toilet. Really, why would I?

The only reason I can think is that the toilet has been struggling to flush a bit. The water in the bowl swirling right up to the rim. It generally does it at the weekend when there seems to be a lot of people at home in the flats. Am I now worrying about the water blocking up in the loo now?

I seem to be spending my days worrying about every little thing and blowing it up out of all proportion. I often wonder if anyone else who is a manic depressive gets this crap in their head. Because I for one would like it removed. It's no wonder the Victorians used dubious methods to try and cure people with mental illnesses. Glad I wasn't born in that era. I'd be a frazzled. (They used electrification treatment for those of you who are too young to remember). Amongst other grizzly methods.

Well how do I follow that?

Funnily enough an innocent little trip to Asda along the canal can bring its share of episodes. I would call them adventures, but these are not.

The canal path at the back of Kurt's is flat and easy enough for me to manoeuvre now that the ground is dry. Normally a quite walk to the supermarket and back, for essential shopping and close enough to get to the Post Office to post my Jewellery packets. (My little creative side business that keeps me in Prosecco and fags)

Today was not one of those days. For some reason, maybe the sun coming out and smiling at us, the place was busier than usual. Barking dogs, children, and mothers with push chairs and crazy Not right.

A Not right is someone who shouts their business to the world in public, in vulgar language. The air around them is blue! They argue about their relationships in public on top note. The male Not right, is riding a bicycle and holding a walking stick. The lady Not right is trying to get away from him. Screaming on top note that she is going to call the police. Why I have no idea.

The first time the Not rights pass me. They pass very closely on each side of me. I am heavily laden with a shopping bag in each hand. The footpath is no more than two meters wide. Frome the edge of the canal to the bushes. It's very tight for three people, a bicycle and a crazy man waving a walking stick around.

I feel dirty as they passed me. Not out of snobbery, may I add. Their language may be blue, their choice of scent is definitely ingrained marijuana. Not rights have no sense of social distancing whatsoever. They're oblivious to others in society. Their conversation regarding, who'd slept with whom, who was a dirty bitch and who wasn't really for other peoples, ears. Lovely! just what you want on a peaceful sunny day walk with the shopping already pulling your elbows to the ground. Not!

Thankfully, the lady Not right or not (A lady) as the conversation has revealed? Walked quickly in front of me and passed where I turned to cross the river at the lock towards home. Phew, glad that was over. No, I spoke too soon their return was announced by the Not right man's loud shouting. More blue air! They turned the corner and were coming straight at me.

I couldn't believe it. My blood turned. I was thinking of ways to get them away from me they were getting too close to me. How to push the Not right on the bike into the canal, was looking like my favourite option. They both felt so threatening and annoying. So rude and inconsiderate. I just wanted them out of the way.

I couldn't believe how angry they made me feel and that I was considering hitting them with my heavy shopping bags too push them into the canal. I actually saw myself doing it and the Not right on the bicycle falling in the canal and not being able to swim in the green murky water.

Shouting with his arms flapping in the air and the woman turning on me. Suddenly she cares about him and doesn't want to call the police.

That brought me back to reality. The Not right lady then shoved passed me then hid behind me and started shouting at him again. Over my shoulder breathing all over my back. Heaven! I turned round with a face of thunder and shouted at her,

"what do you think you are doing trying to hide behind me". She was nearly holding my t-shirt she was that close. I could smell her. Ready to push them both into the canal at this stage whether they could swim or not. What a total Not right.

I'm not sure what came over me. I had just had enough of them. Surprisingly, they both scurried off. I needed a bath. They both stunk of stale marijuana. They had breathed God knows what all over me they were that close. They really freaked me out.

I walked home trying to think what the hell might have happened if I'd pushed them into the canal. Would the Police have come in time to save them? I certainly couldn't with my arthritic feet. The fact that I was actually thinking about it really astounded me.

That's what they call a, near miss, in Health and safety terms. That it certainly was for them.

For me, a very worrying episode, that someone could push me to be so anxious I wanted them in the canal. That is truly scary!

Chapter 34

Total deaths in the UK 7,878
Boris is out of ICU
Ironing and posting.
10th April 2020

The death toll is still rising. Boris Johnson our Prime Minister is out of ICU so luckily, he's not one of them. The thought of having to pick another PM (Prime Minister) is too daunting. He is a good leader and a doer. Less of a politician and more of a man who wants to bring us back to the way the UK was. One country, one people all working together to a common goal. Not a bunch of Not rights worrying about how to stop the country moving forward and creating bad feeling and mayhem just to stop things getting done while the rest of us suffer.

I seem to have accumulated a mountain of ironing. It seriously is a mountain. So high it's driving me nuts walking past it. I need to manage it. Along with all the posting trips to the post office to get rid of my little parcels. I need to allocate posting days. Something to think on.

UK deaths 980 from the 9th total in UK 8,958

11th April 2020

Today was going to be my writing day. No going out. Just chilling and writing. Needless to say, I got distracted. So, what's new? It's me. Why would I expect any less? Even with all this isolation with the Corona V I still seem to let myself get distracted. My Brain is still attempting to multitask. Pure insanity. I know I can't do much without getting tired and exhausted and returning to a dark place. What I can't pinpoint is how much can I do before I should stop.

Being driven is a curse. I have decided. No, correction, it's my curse! Where, once it was my asset to survival and success it is now my nemesis. (Defined by the Oxford dictionary as the inescapable agent of someone's or something's downfall) Sometimes described as the bane of a person's life. It certainly is that! More than a bloody bane. A BBB (Bastard Bloody Bane......)

It certainly is an addiction. Being a smoker and drinker, I have to hold my hands up to that one. That said, taking tablets isn't really my thing. It's much like wearing glasses. I find it a bloody inconvenience.

Many people who are driven are connected to wanting to climb the corporate ladder. The only climbing I wanted to do was mountains since being little and climbing Snowdon with my mother.

I never really saw myself as that corporate person. All I ever wanted was to earn enough money to raise my son and give him a happy life so we could survive. To put enough food on the table and a roof over our heads. There was no plan. There was no help. Maybe it was all done

subconsciously. I never would have imagined that being driven would have brought this Dark illness to my door. I just wanted enough money to live on. Not much to ask. I didn't think then. But now I find I was.

With no family network support from the age of twenty there didn't seem any other alternative.

Total UK deaths 11,329
An increase of 717 from yesterday.
14th April 2020

At 4.30am I am still tossing and turning. What the hell is this all about? I went to sleep dead tired at ten I couldn't even read. My brain is too restless to settle this morning. I didn't want to wake Kurt. So, I creep out of bed in the dark. Using my phone as a torch. Not sure why really, Kurt sleeps like a horse. (No that's cruel) Let's say, not easily woken. That's my PC bit for today.

After finally getting the television (I'm going to call it the TV from now on) set to work. That means it wasn't so loud the neighbours shot out of their beds. It also means I actually got to manoeuvred round the two TV gadgets and got it right. Yeh!! First time for a while.

Kurt has tried to teach me the process of switching the TV on, but I have to admit it's something I am totally crap at. I somehow manage to get no sound, too much sound, one channel and no other. Enough to say it is not my strong point.

Today both Sky News and the BBC are full of how people are coping with lockdown. I have to admit that unlike others I don't find lock down a problem. I'm becoming incredibly happy in my little cocoon of life. That's hardly surprising from someone who struggled to go out

prior to lock down starting.

Kurt and I have discussed that we are sick of not having our freedom to go on little adventures when we want. Like getting in the car and going for a drive. But as they don't sometimes materialise because I become dark and unable I'm used to taking the safe option and stay in. I think cancelling two holidays now and not being able to see my family is kind of taking it toll. But luckily the health and safety of both our families is more important to us to we're happy to see this through to the end.

Like myself , Kurt is also aware that there are people out there who aren't following the rules and are really letting the rest of us down.

I write my shopping list for today. We only need a few things, but I really don't look forward to going out. As I am a soldier of adventure, I will do it. I can do it!

Chapter 34

People Going the Extra Mile

People are jumping up out of the Corona V Pandemic as real superstars. There is no way I could really mention them all. This book would end up as a Pandemic. There are people who can, people who have and people, who have found a need in our changed society and have just gotten on with doing things.

Below is an unusual one I have picked out. This doesn't mean it is the only one. God knows they are not. Every single person who has helped another even in a tiny little way deserves thanks as we all do what we can. However great or small. It all counts in our great humanity family.

So, before I continue, thank you to everyone who has helped, big hugs and kisses and thank you to all those of you who have left us because of their amazing sacrifices.

"For the love of Scrubs" – Extracts taken from their face book site,

This was initially formed by Ashleigh Linsdell after identifying a shortage in supply of scrubs to frontline NHS staff during the Corona V Pandemic. Ashleigh, a nurse who worked forty hours a week and then came home and made scrubs, for her fellow workers, so they didn't run out. Is an amazing character for finding that amount of energy and dedication to her job?

The Facebook group is a platform to enable those who are able to, and would like to contribute towards supplying hospitals local to themselves with scrubs for front line workers.

Some hospitals in the UK are facing a shortage in scrubs and PPE, this means our nurses are not as safe as they should be. Ashleigh set up a face book page to raise £500 toward equipping those who would like to contribute but were not able to make things.

From this 20 scrubs kits were created and distributed as fairly as possible to those who cannot afford to buy their own around the country. Each scrub set requires approximately 3.5m of poly cotton, elastic/ tie waist approximately 83cm elastic.

This small idea snowballing into many Nurses and their families making kits at home with the help of supplies and family. Well done Ashleigh and everyone else who took part.

The total UK deaths 11,329 increase of 717 from yesterday.

17th April 2020

It's 18.50pm Push, push, push, that's what I've had to do to get myself to use my laptop this evening. My brain still thinks it's the morning. You could say I've lost a day. I feel dark. Miserable and completely unable to shake myself out of it. I should have gone to the post office and bank but just couldn't push myself to do it. The sun is shining, I just couldn't push myself to leave the flat. It's beautiful outside.

The darkness had got its hold on me again. I try to shake myself like a dog but nothing. I've had a nap at twelve for three hours with the intention of being refreshed and ready to crack on with my book.

I just can't switch my positive side on. Three bloody days of this and writing notes on scraps of paper. Nothing seems to make me happy, yet I have nothing to be unhappy about. I spoke to my doctor yesterday and he said many people who had been fine before had dropped back into the darkness. I hate it, no I don't hate it, I don't hate anyone. I just hate the way this makes me feel. The Fact that I can't shake it.

The doctor says he can't up the medication. I didn't ask him to. I am making myself write this to

218

see if that shakes me out of it. It so annoying when I have so much to write and so much research.

I have endless diaries on the bookshelf in my office. I started to write them over the years, travel journals, daily diaries, notes, travel files, endless research materials, and relationship diaries all started with the best intentions. Many stopped because of my past Dark moments. I just couldn't put what was really happening down on paper.

Well from now on it's going to be my life's work to get all the painful memories and funny adventures out. If the medications won't help me anymore and will only keep me calm, I really have to keep pushing myself until it kills or cures me. There seems to be no other way.

By the time I wait for the treatment from the hospital I fear I will have lost the plot totally. They said it could be months a year. I have to take control of stopping this. If I can.

I've tried the sleeping, relaxation therapy, thinking adventures and non-adventures through. Drinking alcohol, that doesn't seem to touch me, just wakes me up early to go to the loo.

I have so much in my head I don't know if getting it all out will help or make things worse. But I think that is a risk I am prepared to take. Every time something pops up in my brain, I need to explore it or write it down now. There is no other option open to me now. I will need to explore it and see how it goes however silly or painful. My brain is obviously trying to communicate with me. I know it's a risk, to do this in an uncontrollable environment but I don't feel like I have any other option. Once the help channel is opened up to me again, we will have lots to talk about.

Here we go. I just jumped up and cleared the dishes off the drainer and put Kurt's soup on for tea. I tidy everywhere up so he can't tell how dark my day has been. When he comes in and ask me about my day, I will tell him it has been fine. I can tell he's started worrying about me. So now I'm masking it a little. Not easy.

I've been going off to bed early when I've been exhausted. Which is something we never do alone. We always go together. But now that I know tiredness is one of my triggers I have to rest when it beckons.

Total UK deaths 15,464 an increase of 888 from yesterday.

18th April 2020

Woke up feeling fine, I think! I really don't know what fine is anymore. A little dazed dizzy took my medication but don't seem to be coming round. Time to shake myself. I did tell Kurt I would go out with him to the shops. But that's not going to happened. It's the last thing I feel like doing.

I receive the post and true to form another government department tips me over the edge into darkness.

Yesterday I contacted the Council of Chesterfield Borough to confirm I had moved, on the 6th of April, as I hadn't heard anything from them from prior contact. They have replied to me to tell me that I owe them £258.10 for last year's rates which was the benefit amount they had allowed me after so many changed decisions. I think a total of five separate ones were sent to me.

Who ever read my letter obviously didn't read it properly? They totally missed the point that I had moved in with Kurt as I was no longer able to look after myself at my other address where I lived alone as I was totally isolated from shops and people. Was it because I'd said he had been helping me while I was living there?

They have totally misunderstood the previous relationship or are they are just hell bent on saving every penny they can. One thing is for sure, all this talk in the media and everywhere about helping people with mental illnesses whether from Corona V or a previous condition. No one really gives a shit.! Its all a load of crap that makes people and organisations sound good.

The news is currently full of people telling you about all the help you can get to lessen people's anxiety. All this letter has achieved is raised my heart palpitations even higher than before and caused me to stress about having to write to them yet again when all they had to do was check where

Kurt was paying his rates before for one address and myself from another.

Bloody shoddy workmanship that's what I call it. Why do they do this shit to you. Do they think that because I have been honest and told them of my move that they can presume I must have been cheating? How bloody dare they. Don't they know that a person can only pay rates at one house at the time? Is, there any wonder people like me don't want to open their mail?

I really thought I was opening something which I had done correctly. Then bang they hit me hard again. Well, writing to them yet again will have to wait for tomorrow. I just can't deal with this now. I feel sick to my stomach. Bastards, I hope they are happy. I have to lay down and take more red pills to calm my heart down before I explode.

Councils have just been given an extra £1.6bn cash to help them deal with the immediate impact of the pandemic, including helping rough sleepers off the streets and schemes to assist extremely vulnerable people shielded in their own homes.

I was extremely vulnerable in my own home. I was at my wits end being on my own and incapable of going far or doing much. Frightened of going on the bus or in a taxi to go shopping. But because I did something positive about it and made a life changing decision to move in with Kurt and make life easier for both of us, I now get penalised.

A person gives me a home and makes me feel safe and does the shopping, cooking and give me someone to cuddle when I am thoroughly prickled up with stress and goes to work to keep the countries bins working so we don't end up with trash on our streets. Thanks, world for nothing.

Know something world of bureaucrats who adore paperwork. I will survive. Not matter what it takes. I will survive!! This book will be written, and it will be one of many. No matter what you throw at my mental illness. It can't get any worse. As Doctor Ali says, I'm going to rest!

20th April 2020

Here's my answer to the person from the council who cost me 3 days of total darkness and completely ruined my weekend. I thought long and hard about it. No that's wrong. The letter's words have been engrained in my brain all weekend. Making me want to bite my nails so much. But I wouldn't. (The last time I did that I was thirteen years old) I never really knew why I did it when someone asked me. It certainly made me stop I felt so embarrassed.

Maybe now I do. I was having anxiety attacks then. Maybe my knuckles next time will do less damage. I have to answer this council person and let them know how they've made me feel. They can't keep doing this to people. Some, people in these offices really don't know how to check their letters before they send them, or they are working from a predetermined template and don't adjust it accordingly. They seem to be in such a rush they really don't care.

The Queens 94th Birthday

No celebrations due to the Corona V

449 deaths total in the UK its finally dropping.

21st April 2020

9.00am Today I woke up without the Darkness. Yeh… its finally lifted. I can't wait to sit down and write. I can't explain how happy that makes me. I don't dilly dally in bed I'm up making my coffee tiding the kitchen and out comes my laptop. All that before I even hear the figures.

My Red notebook is out, and I can't get my thoughts out quick enough. I can't believe how much is coming out of my brain. It's great to be back.

The nightmares last night were all about Ken Kelly, Che's dad. Three times I woke up and each time when I feel back to sleep the dream started again. It was horrible, frightening.

Initially I found myself in a house much like the one we used to live in at Ashgate Valley road near the river. Only it wasn't. As I walk through the house there is no one there. I'm scared of what or who I will find there but my feet make me continue. There are multiple rooms added on to the house and it resembles a long veranda with plants growing through the windows and floors with rooms off it. Each door opens into a smelly smoke filled room of chaos. Sheets strewn everywhere and dense marijuana smoke. That dank stale smell everywhere. But totally deserted.

I walk through to an overgrown garden. Fight my way through to the other side where there is a gate. That is my escape plan. I have to leave. I don't want to be found here.

As I go through the gate, I can go up a very steep hill or right on the flat road neither of which I can recognise. I choose the hilly route. Why when I have a poorly foot which hurts most when it's going uphill. It makes no sense, but I push myself to keep going as if someone is behind me. Chasing me, frightening me. I turn there is no one there. I wake up before I reach the top to see what is there.

I go to the toilet and return to a lovely cuddle and another wonderful sleep. This is very unusual for me. Usually I would now be tossing and rethinking the dream trying to work out what it was all about.

This time I enter the house the same way, through the back but I walk straight into an open plan living room similar to the one we had forty years ago. There are strangers sat around the dining table. Dirty scruffy strangers stinking of ingrained marijuana. The air is dense and stale. There are beer bottles and reefer ends all over the table. They look up at me with no signs of recognition. They carry on their conversation. Their lips move but I hear nothing.

I go past them and open the door at the end. I am in the same veranda type extension as before. This time there are people in the rooms. A sleep, or hi as a kite. Talking all sorts of crap. Barely acknowledging me as I open the doors. Just looking at me with some strange half happy

half distant look. I carry on to the end. This time someone is following me. I spend up to get towards the end door. I need to escape. Then I stop. I need to talk to someone and ask where Ken is?

The person pursuing me is pleased I've stopped. He smiles. I don't know him. He knows me. I think really hard but there is no recognition. I don't have a light bulb moment. Just a vague look of trying to place someone. He asks me if I'm Veronica. I say I am. I ask him when Ken will be back. He says later. To wait he would be happy to see me. I doubt that.

He asks me to leave my mobile number so Ken can ring me. I don't think so. I don't need a drug enthused, control freak who still thinks he owns me and can terrorise me to come to be ringing me. I question why I am there. I do want to talk to Ken, but I don't know what about. I pull a confused face. I say I'm sorry and I continue walking through the wilderness of a garden.

Moving the long weeds out of my way. I get to the path this time I see familiar lights of a shop and a bus stop. It's the Spar petrol station I walk towards it and I feel Kurt trying to unravel himself from me to get up without disturbing me. The dream stops.

I turnover the other way and the dream starts again. I'm at the back door going in, boldly this time. Feeling more confident about what to expect. I have a purpose. I don't know what it is, but something is pushing me to find out. I want to get to the bottom of it. I must be subconsciously thinking it will help me. I get to the dining room and walk straight past the table full of people. The atmosphere is even denser there are more people there. It's like something from an old movie where they are playing poker. Full of tension. Something makes me turn round. I ask is Ken in. Someone looks towards a skeleton at the table. I point and say

"No. It can't be him." I look again.

It looks like a skeleton with a long beard and that charismatic smile I used to fall for so often. Not today. I shake myself. He is still there he starts to speak. The vision is shattered. I wake up.

Not upset and agitated as these dreams would normally leave me but refreshed.

It shocks me. I really don't know what this dream has achieved. Maybe as my brother said recently. My relationship with him did more damage than I was aware. I thought after he'd died a few weeks ago I would get closure from his cremation. With no councillor to ask for help or an explanation I can only think it must have done some good. So, I am grateful for that. It just remains to see if the dream returns. Hopefully not. It would be great to be able to shut that door. Time will tell..

Today is our wonderful Queen Elizabeth 11s Birthday. Unfortunately, there will be no flights past or family celebrations. I am really proud of her. I bet after all she went through, during and after the second world war she never expected to see the country in the place it is now. Still her being with us and her lovely speech the other week really made us feel like we were all in it together. As we are. She and her family are all self-isolating. I would say for her and her wonderful husband Prince Philip, a much needed rest after all those years of traveling and smiling.

Chapter 35

The Good, The Bad and the Ugly.

This is where I really need to share a tirade with you all. I have been so filled with pride at the way our nation has responded to the lockdown. Some people's actions actually bring me to tears. However, no matter who difficult and however hard our Government has tried to deal with the unknown entities of this unprecedented virus to keep us safe, it's never enough for some.

Poor Boris Johnson has run himself to the ground to try and balance everything that has been thrown at him since he became Prime Minister a few weeks ago. The Brexit Mess (TBM) and the Corona V.

For a few short weeks while all the political parties were re: writing themselves and licking their battle worn paws wondering what they had done so wrong for the people to turn to Boris. The news has been quiet and peaceful of all the infighting.

Initially stunned by Boris's win and thrown by the outbreak of the Corona V in China. The world was watching someone else and blaming them for life's problems. Phew …. what a bloody relief. My ears couldn't stand any more of it. The same rehashed shit time and time again. I was sick of shouting abuse at the television set.

UK Politics was waiting for the labour party to choose a new leader and get rid of the extremely negative Mr Corbin. Attacking politicians for the sake of it and tearing our country to pieces with his hateful ideology.

After years of political public, arguing and point scoring it has felt like the United Kingdom is

finally, at peace. Even our Journalists are quiet. Good. (Kindness and Unity- The team is back!)

The news is now all about how we can help each other and cope with this new world we now need to live in to protect our human race. Filled with as much information as we can be given to help us make the right decisions to help ease the unique situation, we find ourselves in.

The UK has suddenly found itself, full of all the good things people are doing to help each other to get through this Corona V. The other politicians can't find much to pontificate about and be negative because if their honest they really don't know enough about the virus. And why should they? We've never been through something like this before so best not to say too much and look foolish.

Finally, all our politicians, even the Scottish First Minister, Nicola Sturgeon, has stopped banging on about Scotland leaving the UK. Thank goodness. I was really beginning to think I should send her a wine cork to put in her mouth to shut her up (sorry that was too rude) and see if she saw the funny side of it. Nicola had really become like a stuck record. Banging her drum relentlessly.

Obviously, she is passionate about Scotland leaving the UK, but seriously woman, change the subject. We as the UK don't want it to happen so please get the message. It won't happen in this parliament. We want to work together as a team. Why can't you get it? Seriously, and work together. There's been enough division for the past three years.

I often wonder if any of you politicians out there know how many of us switch off our Television (TV) sets when you start with the same old same old. It really is getting to be the topic of conversation. I'm not surprised Boris Johnson got voted in. He's the only person the rest

of us could honestly relate too. He made us feel he had our country's interest at heart and would make us great again instead of being laughed at all over the globe for behaving like fish wives in public and losing all our self-respect as a nation.

Is there any wonder no one in Europe took our Brexit negotiations seriously? The whole world could see how divided and undecided everyone in politics was in the UK. You all created mass confusion. A creation of power hungry politicians. There really is no other explanation for it. You politicians were ducking and diving and jumping and sinking from one ship to another.

Totally confusing the UK family and when you started back tracking and changing your minds that was the end for us all. None of you seemed brave enough to stand on your own two feet and support the publics vote only Boris.

You are after all servants of the people and they had voted. As distasteful as that was for some of us. A vote is a vote and we are a democracy. Politicians who tried to change that vote and wanted it re voted were in danger of destroying our democracy and questions every UK citizens reason for voting in any election or bi election. The ballot box is sacred. Once counted it is the outcome and can't be changed because we don't like the result.

We all only have one focus now. Just sticking to what the Government is doing to help put us on the right footing to fight together and get this mammoth logistical task of putting so many different extra desperately needed supply chains in place. Get businesses in place to change what they're creating to make the products we need to protect our National Health Service (NHS) and us from the virus. For once the focus is in the correct place. Let's keep it there and keep us all safe.

Quite frankly if we don't there won't be enough space to bury us all. Some countries are already struggling. Come on guys let's do this together. There are bound to be some mistakes. No one knows the real answer. If you want to be critical wait until you have all the facts. Please don't distract for the sake of juggling for position. Your position in politics doesn't matter to us, our lives do!

The government can only focus on the information they are given. They are guided by experts, and not by the what ifs. As cruel as it may seem there has to be priorities in these situations.

Not only has our government been focusing on the health of the nation but also our pockets. Showing businesses how they can survive differently and protect people's income. Creating a change in production and producing the things our country doesn't currently produce which we desperately need to get through this Pandemic.

Given it may have been overrun with help offers from various small businesses maybe there aren't enough people to cope with the requests in the government offices. Any business would always focus on its current supply chain first and then build new local ones in tandem. It's alright

buying things from abroad but the delivery timelines aren't always an advantage. Especially when the whole world is being supplied from the same suppliers. It's like lots of screaming kids wanting the same ice cream when there is only one left.

A country which has recently been in lock down itself is bound to have delivery issues. Some common sense is required and redirected to enable our increase in need fulfilment.

During the 2nd World War, our factories had to change what they were making, and workforces had to change. It's wonderful that we have been able to adapt so well and will keep doing so to help out.

It will be interesting to see if we make use of this new spread of local suppliers when this is all over. But that's for another book. I think.

The Government is still getting revenue to businesses and giving work to those who are able, safely within what they are advised is safe, for those who are still in work.

For a long time as a country we have been focused in a different direction. Always moving towards the cheapest labour and the cheapest marketplace. Never really thinking the unthinkable. What if we as a nation had to be self-sufficient? Where was our contingency plan? What if we can't import people and goods from abroad to sustain our standard of life? What have we got here that we could survive?

Well lots of innovative young people have shown us that masks and gowns are easy enough to make. When we are in a desperate position there is the willingness to help. Why, I wonder was the workforce or businesses in the UK, not so eager to produce these previously, when they were

not so desperately needed. Were the margins so thin that businesses can't enter into those markets normally?

Maybe we should. It's obvious we have the skills. We also have people who want to work or need work which we need to help to get back into work. It's surly logical if there is a market opening and a workforce, we should be grasping these opportunities. Just a thought from a crazy woman.

Chapter 36

Sickness Benefit V Survival

When I was eighteen and left home, I worked in a fish and chip shop to survive. Believe me it wasn't my first choice. Urgh…. People on the bus going home used to ask me if I worked in a Fish and Chip shop? The smell was the giveaway. How embarrassing at the age of eighteen to be asked that. But needs must and I needed money to subsidise my education and survive.

My bedsit rent was only £4.00 a week, but without work there would have been no bedsit.

After a few months of being there I contracted a rash. A very ugly red rash which itched all day. As I was working with food I was asked to go to the doctors. I had contracted scabies, something I had never heard of. Consequently, I wasn't allowed to go to work the heat from the oil vats was exacerbating it.

Great I asked how had I got it? I had no idea. Being naive and young. I was told it could be from the blankets from the new flat. So, I got rid of all the bedding everything had to go. Expensive but necessary. That done I was still itching. The doctor couldn't understand it. He asked if I had a partner? I did. PX3 He suggested I treat him with the lotion as well. He wasn't amused. Once he was treated for a few days he too started to recover as did we both.

Then week six it came back again. The doctor did suggest that it could be sexually transmitted. What a way to find out your true love is a cheating bastard. While you're out working hard to make ends meet, he was shagging a barmaid friend of mine. Don't you love them. I was horrified, disgusted, felt filthy. Threw the dirty bug ridden bastard out and the bugs went with him.

There is a moral here somewhere, but that too is for another book. (I have too many here to list)

My point is, forty three years ago when I went off sick the government allowance was £5.00 a week to live on when sick. That left me with £1.00 to survive on. Not easy. To be fair you could buy a lot of food for a £1.00. Students staple diets are always similar to that of a long elastic band. It can be stretched as far as needed.

There were no other benefits I knew of and I couldn't work anywhere until I was clear. So, I learnt my lesson the hard way. Not to depend on anyone but myself for money to survive. Hence it never entered my head not to work throughout my life. I just pushed and pushed myself so there was always enough.

A hard lesson to learn at eighteen years. It all stood me in good stead for the future battles ahead. It could have been the start of my driven behaviour. Until I get the therapy needed, I won't know.

Chapter 37

Pensioners lead through Inspiration.

The world feels like a much better place now. People are helping each other and not just thinking about themselves. If this is only the tip of the iceberg our wonderful country needs to push it into the right direction so let's embrace it today.

Captain Thomas Moore, a ninety nine years old man, who served in the second world war in Burma, where my father served, has shown the world how his wish to raise a small thank you for the NHS who cared for him can snowball. Such a simple kindness has provoked so many to donate because of this man's courage, wonderful selfless smile and magnanimous appreciation for all the people who have donated.

His mission, was a simple target of £1,000 to give to NHS Charities Together by completing laps of his garden, with the help of his walker, to be achieved before his 100th birthday.

Tom started his thank you walk on Good Friday after TV and Newspaper coverage Tom smashed his target with over 1.5 million people from all over the world making generous donations to his fundraising page.

He blew his target within a matter of days but continued to walk on and really inspire our nation. He also made a number 1 hit single with Michael Ball during lockdown of their version of , "You'll never walk alone." He was truly an inspiration to many. An amazing man.

Captain Tom raised £32,796,696 million online and £6,173,838.31 from Gift Aid when his just giving page was closed. An unimaginable amount that will do so much good.

His efforts inspired a 90 year old Highland lady, Margaret Payne to climb the equivalent of a 2,398ft Scottish mountain in her own home, by climbing the stairs to help raise £10,000 for the NHS and a local hospice, in the fight against coronavirus.

Margaret Payne is making 282 trips up her household steps to climb the height of Suilven which is a whopping 2,398ft.

Extract taken from the Scottish Herald.

"She started the challenge on Easter Sunday, and it is expected it will take her around two months to reach her goal height.

Mrs Payne said: "I have now lived in the Highlands for over 40 years and I would like to raise funds to support the NHS in particular at this difficult time. It is not the first time Margaret will have climbed the mountain she first accomplished the feat at aged 15 in 1944 with her sister Elizabeth, when the pair were evacuated to Glencanisp, Lochinver during the war.

She now lives in Ardvar, Sutherland, and was inspired to take on the challenge to raise funds for the NHS during the coronavirus pandemic and also for Highland Hospice.

The hospice cared for her husband, Jim, who died on Christmas day last year."

As of today (30/5/2020), Margaret has raised £410,972.28 including gift aid.

There are so many wonderful acts of kindness being performed today I could fill my book with amazing people but alas I would never get it finished.

So, to you all the biggest thank you.

Even those who are doing it silently, who don't want publicity or any reward they just want to help. More unsung heroes. I know you are out there, and I thank you on behalf of everyone.

Farmers are selling fruit and vegetable boxes over the internet and meat boxes for those who are struggling to get out so they delivery. How wonderful is this? Why can't we do it all the time. Why do we let supermarkets take over?

I've noticed alcohol has shot up in price over the last few weeks. Yet on the internet private sellers are struggling and the prices are comparable and from what I've seen the portions are very generous.

What is this nonsense about perfectly shaped vegetables and fruit? Where the hell did that ever come from? Seriously people. If you've ever grown your own perfectly shaped fruit and vegetables, you'll know it doesn't happen that often. In fact, I would be suspicious of where it's been grown if it were too perfect. Fruits on market stalls and from farms are the freshest and so delicious. Who even looks at their shape? Well I'm sorry if you do. Please get a life. I've been too busy in mine to notice.

Chapter 38

The UGLY's (Useless Greedy Low Life Yobs) but the tide is turning.

Too much political pressure and shareholder pressure has stopped us thinking like the great British nation we are. The divide which some of our politicians have jumped on to divide us has gone too far. The anger towards others in our communities has caused some hateful jealous wrongly informed individuals.

The people on social media who have wished Boris dead have, shown us just how far some of these UGLY people will go. On the other side other people haven't been afraid of these social demons who think they can hurt anyone. People have started to name and shame them without fear to stop them.

Thankfully, it's started to work. Social media has stopped people selling toilet rolls for £26 each. Why would anyone be so greedy to do that? Greedy UGLY's people with no social conscious. No compassion for others. I believe in the free market as much as anyone else but that is UGLY.

I had plenty of toilet rolls myself, so when I saw some in the shops, I bought some for friends with children who were struggling to get enough because of the supermarkets initial rationing when they had some. How difficult is that to do. I even offered to share what we have until they could get some.

When I last checked Corona V doesn't cause diarrhoea so why the bog roll obsession!

If this pandemic has taught us anything. We had got too complacent and used to people taking advantage of our marketplaces. Marketing is a wonderful tool. It can turn the simplest of items into something that looks like a tasty expensive item. Purely by how it is packaged. Simply put, if you put a Harrods wrapper, label, or box on something the price magically increases.

We sadly chose to pay the price for all of the items fancy wrapping. The fact is we only get what we pay for in life. If we want a Rolls Royce vegetable, we have to pay the price with all its fancy wrappings. If we want them wobbly, smelling fresh and tasty in a paper bag we can enjoy the taste of real food.

Once we have prepared our food or cooked it, does the original shape really matter? Surly the majority of the time it doesn't. We buy with our eyes not with smell and taste. One of my favourite experiences is buying fruit and vegetables is on Spanish outdoor markets. The attraction is only partially visual.

Each stall holder will cut up their wares and encourages the customer to taste. Try not buying a peach that smells and tastes like it's just been picked. Licking its fresh juices still on your fingers.

Who wouldn't buy one? Olives sampled from a jar infused with its various oils and fresh herbs. There really is no other way to buy food.

Even dubious friends, when invited for a Mediterranean lunch comment on the freshness of all its ingredients. No packaging, no prefect sizing just food straight from its source.

As newer marketplaces are opening up everyone is getting a chance to sell their products to all of us. The farmer will deliver his fresh produce to your door. I guarantee it will last longer ,

taste better and swell like food should do. Something, which seems to have been lost in fancy packaging and shelf life.

Let's learn a lesson from this please. Fresh and local is beautiful no matter what shape it is.

Two of the reasons I didn't become a Journalist, forty years ago, were one, the salary was too low to bring up a child on my own and two, when I started to explore the world of journalism I was shocked to find that the focus of editors was more on digging out bad news stories instead of celebrating good news stories, family experiences, and feel good community stories.

These editors and journalists who allowed themselves to be driven by selling newspapers full of negativity, some while not being true to themselves have contributed to the world of negativity we now live in. Whether it be intentional or not. The focus on leaving important words/facts out of a story and the power of suggestion have followed many through life. UGLY.

Unfortunately, people believed in what they read in the newspapers. Why shouldn't they? The fact that conversations have been manipulated or information taken out of context to suit a purpose never crosses most people's minds. Brexit was a typical recent example of this.

Today, Journalists have the greatest opportunity to rise and share good information, positive stories and cover all helpful avenues people desperately want to hear from. Granted we had three weeks of a lull of negativity. Not sure if that was the shock of Corona v entering our shores or the lack of people in the opposition to poke and create havoc with. From my perspective it was a lovely peaceful time with people trying to help each other. A time of good positive journalism.

As social media and some news channels took up the gauntlet and spread good news it was a pleasure to watch the programmes or people using their initiative to help anyone they could and support the NHS.

Bad. (Brainless and Deranged)

These are the element in society who don't give a shit and clearly say so at every opportunity they can. They are BAD. They don't care about others only think of themselves. Push past you on the canal toll path, shove past you in supermarkets, cough at you to provoke a reaction. They don't want to queue they would rather shout and threaten staff in shops and threaten their families.

To all you BAD people out there, I say.

"Think before you speak and do." Imagine this scenario.

"What would you do if the hospital refused you treatment because you caught the virus out of sheer arrogance and stupidity? I certainly would not help you."

Enough of my rambling back to the present.

Chapter 38

Strange Smells!
616 deaths (lowest weekday figure in 3 weeks.)
Total death for UK 18,738
24th April 2020

It's 3.50am, OMG Kurt, reign it in will you. Tossing and turning and pumping for the last two hours. My bedroom does not smell like the sweet haven it usually is. I am scratching my head trying to think what I have given him to eat that could have caused all this tummy disruption.

After much thinking it can only be one of two items. One, my dearest beloved had a couple of Stella cans, his liquid food, and Two, baked potatoes with baked beans. Both I suppose lethal in their own way.

Strange because Kurt is notorious for his very gentle manly noises, but I do not normally smell anything. Others have been rude enough to mentioned it when we have been out. God bless brothers and sisters. Me I have never noticed a thing.

I am just wondering if my nostrils are finally smelling something that has been there all the time?

247

For years now, since I had a fall in my cottage garden, some seventeen years ago. I have not been able to smell anything or extraordinarily little. Slowly, over the last couple of years, some

pure smells or extraordinarily strong perfumes have been gradually breaking through. But nothing unpleasant.

Often, when a woman has worn a scent which does not mix well with her body chemicals and sprayed it in the lady's loo, I have felt a little overcome by it temporarily.

Like many adventures in my life the fall was a strange episode and one I dearly paid for. To, this day, I still cannot remember anything about it. (One of my many little 'garden' adventures to my son's dismay. Each with its own story.)

It was my last job of the afternoon before I had to go in to clean up to go out to dinner. One minute I was standing with a claw hammer on top of some stone steps in my garden, poised for action (About six feet off the ground). To try to pull out an old horse harness hook, which was rusting to bits and really annoying me.

As it was strongly embedded into the stonework at the side of the house. (It was getting in the way of a water collection project I was installing.) And why would it not be after all it had held horses there for the last hundred and fifty years. The next minute I woke up on a stone path in my garden, six foot lower down. I do not know how long I was there.

In fact, I was dazed and totally out of it. I somehow took myself up the remaining stairs into the house and off to bed. Holding the back right of my head. I locked all the doors after me and snuggled up in my comfy bed. Not sure how I got up the stairs to bed, but I was there.

It was lovely and peaceful given that my husband had just gone off to Spain the day before to play golf and I had the week off to do some jobs and some catching up with my family.

I was due to meet my brother Pete for dinner that evening at seven so when I was woken up by the distant ringing of the phone. It was like a musical sound ringing in the remoteness somewhere far away. It took me a while to realise what it was.

My head still bewildered I did not connect the two. I let it ring a few times then decided I should answer it. I must have sounded like a drunken woman. My coordination was all over the place. The phone was right next to the bed. I dropped the receiver. My brother asked he if I was

drunk? Well that does not say much for my reputation does it? But maybe he knows me too well. I said no, but I was feeling strange and my head was hurting, but I cannot remember why. I explained that one minute I was in the garden doing a job, the next I woke up with a headache and a hammer in my hand. I do not know how long I had been lying there.

249

Then I felt my head and it was damp. I turned to look at my damp hand and the pillow and all the bedding were covered in blood. I felt sick. I tried to get up and go to the loo. I struggled dripping blood all the way on the fawn hall carpet and marking all the cream hall walls with bloody fingers.

I was holding the phone all the time trying to talk to my brother. He said when I did not turn up to fetch him, he thought I must have started early. (Drinking he meant. Me being partial to a bottle of Peroni or Prosecco while gardening on a sunny day.) I might have been in better shape if I had.

No, I had had some sort of accident by the looks of things. My brother told me he was going to call an ambulance and would be with me as soon as he could from Salford. I was not making much sense. No nice dinner out then I took it.

He and the ambulance driver arrived at the same time. Good job too. I had gone back to lay in bed as I felt comfy there and just wanted to sleep. Pete opened the front door (Luckily, he had a spare key) and the paramedics flew upstairs to find me laid in all this blood on my bed. Mumbling nonsense and wanting to sleep. Which we all know is not what you do when you have a head injury.

Typical me. But honestly that is how I felt, totally zonked out with no memory of anything. No ambulance trip, no tests nothing.

Peter tells me Bolton hospital were amazing. They went into action straight away, MRI'd my brain, scull whatever they do. X rayed my body to make sure nothing else was damaged.

Miraculously not. I was just sleepy. Finally, when all the testes were finished, I was allowed to go to sleep. I was not in any pain. I was kept in hospital for six days for observation. I do not remember much about the tests and the doctors running around trying to keep me awake while they were assessing me.

What I do remember is being some sort of hell hole of noise where I just wanted to cuddle up in their not so comfortable beds and snuggle. The nurses and tea ladies would insist on waking me up for 6.00am phone calls from my, soon to be X husband and cups of Tea which I did not drink. I did not know which was worse.

The X husbands insincere phone calls waking me out of a beautiful sleep so he would not miss his early Tee off start at golf. Or the endless times I had to tell the geriatric Tea lady I only drank coffee or water. I can still hear her voice saying, 'tea with sugar is good for shock.'

I spent four days minging laying on the bed in the same clothes I went into hospital in blood stained and totally minging. Pete came to see me every day religiously and so did Gillian my friend from the pub across the road from my house. She was looking after my cat, who she was allergic to? The things friends do for you when they really have too.

I was beginning to notice that I wasn't smelling like the fresh Chanel Girl I usually did. I did mention to Gillian that I had not had a wash, brushed my hair or cleaned my teeth since I had been admitted. I really wanted a wash. I had only been allowed to have a commode to have a

wee.

Gillian agreed to bring me a bag with some bathroom bits in and some pyjamas. Anything would be better than these bloodstained clothes and this minging smell. Which I could not seem to define.

During my times in the hospital when I was on my own. I felt like everyone was waiting for some reaction from me. While I was simply happy to sleep it off, they seemed intent on trying to feed me and get some reactions from me.

"I am sorry guys I was on another planet."

The following visiting time, Gill brought me my bag of goodies. All I had to do was get myself to the bathroom. As I was under observation, my bed was right next to the ward double doors. So that adventure should be easy for me to accomplish. I waited until Gill had gone then said I wanted to go for a shower and clean up. Not my best idea.

I was soon to find out why I was under observation. Bear in mind I still could not remember anything nor had any concept of time and I only wanted to sleep. I did not, want to eat and only sipped water in the absence of Coffee.

I was wheelchaired to the shower room, come toilet room with my bag of goodies and a towel.

The excitement of being in clean heaven was short lived. The minute I got out of the wheelchair and into the room I left the door open as instructed and began to get my stuff ready. My Chanel No.5 soap was beckoning. Heaven I would soon smell like normal again. I slowly got undressed and put one foot into the shower. Into the lovely warm cleansing water, I then proceeded to projectile vomit all over the shower cubicle.

Bloody wonderful. I was so shocked I pulled the red cord for help. I really did not know what the bloody hell was happening to me. The nurse came and asked me what was wrong. Seriously! Urgh… As if she could not smell it. If I smelt bad before this was the icing on the cake!

"Oh," she said, that's good, the shock has finally come out of you. We've been waiting for that."

Really shame you did not share it with me or warn me it might happen. When I got over that adventure I said, I would sort myself out and sit back in the chair when I was done.

It took me longer than I expected as I was in terribly slow in cautious mode. But I did succeed.

Completely exhausted, I was taken back to my bed and feel asleep. Hard work vomiting and cleaning up. But wonderful to be clean. Hair washing I had to be gentle as there was no cut as such. God knows where all the blood came from. I never asked. Too traumatic to know. I guess.

My son was away working in Dublin. Just as well really. He always dreaded my house renovation adventures and rightly so this time. He wasn't particularly pleased that I hadn't rung

him and told him what had happened. Going forward the expectation was I would share these episodes with my son no matter what. I promise I will. I was only trying to save you pain and worry darling. XX

Chapter 40

Conclusion to Surviving Madness

Stage One Nearly Over.

When I started writing this book it was intended to be my account of turning sixty and the discovery of the depth of my mental illness along with the impact on my life and earning ability.

It all started as scraps of post its for me to be able to explain to Doctors and the benefit people what I was going through as I couldn't remember from one minute to the next what was happening to me.

I never imagined how much my world and the rest of mankind's worlds could change over a twelve month period. So many people are suffering with isolation and the situation they find themselves in due to Corona V. Something I treasure.

My isolation enables me to hide the Dark days. The one big difference between the world's population suffering from anxiety and depression and myself is, I welcome it! The majority of people seem to be struggling with it. I see it as my safe zone.

Before I can move on to the next stage of my recovery, I feel I need to pull together all the things

I have learned from the past twelve months and produce some sort of action plan. Lessons learned if you like and how to deal with things going forward.

I started this a few days ago then lost the plot. Not unusual as you now realize. My brain does what it wants and revisits my past life often. The flash backs to my past are getting ever more

vivid.

I got as far as setting up a daily plan of waking up and eating, showering and agreeing what I could realistically manage. So let's explore my future goals.

Action Plan.

To maintain the wellness stage, I have achieved I think I need to evaluate what I am capable of and what exhausts me if I am to find any kind of balance or happiness in life. To eliminate the Darkness coming back I need to have safe warnings and obey the triggers and signs. I acknowledge that this is the completion of the first stage and I still have many stages to go. How many no one knows. Only time will tell. It all depends on what life throws at me.

I can only write for a couple of hours a day. That is a complete given.

That does not mean I cannot write for longer. It means that if I do write for longer, I will exhaust myself as I am a driven person and I will go to sleep. (Over my computer or to bed) This is my Driven Demon (DD) which if I am to move forward and survive this illness and get back on my feet, I must find a way to control.

My biggest failure is putting too much energy into doing something and pushing myself to the absolute limit. If I put too much energy into one thing, I cannot do another. That is as good as it

gets, and I have to accept that. So, the choice is simple. I have to organise my writing and other activities into bit size chunks.

Anything stressful, like writing a letter, in answer to benefit issues or other matters which

the author of the letter has got their facts wrong. Any letter which triggers my Dark days because just reading it makes me angry. These triggers will any others, I will need to make a list of and try and learn to manage them. I usually put them to one side until I can face opening them as I dread what some of them will say.

If I do anything which causes my body pain, like walking upstairs or to the Post Office

which is up a steep hill it will zap my much needed energy. If I go for a little walk or do any activity where I will experience pain in my feet or back, then I cannot stand up properly and do the ironing when I get home. Ironing has to be performed sitting or doing one piece at the time and then resting. You can guess how long I need to finish it all.

I am told that ironing sheets is not necessary. Well as long as I can I want to wake up with fresh sheets smelling of Lenor and ironing. What can I say, some things are really worth having? Changing the bed and going up and down stairs to the bedroom completely zaps me of all energy so I have to rest. Talk about doing one job at a time. This often infuriates me as I don't feel I've done enough to exhaust, myself so much and it really infuriates me when I have to sit down and rest. I feel like an old woman.

When I go shopping, I will have put myself through too much pain standing and moving.

Whether I am queuing or studying what I want to buy. I also get Dark moments when someone is dancing around me. With no thought of others some people are so bloody impatient and get so

close to you to try and get something without any thought for social distance. They make you feel like you are in their way. Is there any wonder it takes me an hour to buy a few things? They piss me off so much I forget something become confused and go to the next isle. Then I have to go back again. I sometimes have to circle the supermarket several times before I get all the supplies on my list.

It's like going round a roundabout in a car at the end of the Champs Elysees and not being able to decide which exit I need so I go round again. Too much pressure in too much chaos.

There must be a way for me to balance the housework and washing so that domestic jobs

do not pile up and cause me untoward stress. If I allow jobs to pile up or if the Dark days get to me and I let jobs pile up, I need to get back on track slowly. Again, bit by bit is the only way. Every time I walk past a pile of washing, I stress out. If I try to catch up all at once, I end up straight back in bed totally zapped of energy.

To gain maximum sleep at night I need to read a relaxing book. Something quick reading

with large print. Something that does not strain my eyes. Girly or of real interest. Anything too intense or that jumps around from one year to another and has multiple plots exhausts me

and can cause my nightmares by triggering my past. The slightest similarity to something from my past seems to pull something out of the inner depths of my crazy brain.

I often feel as though as soon as I find something to help relax me it stimulates my brain to further havoc. There is no beating this madness. But I will!

I go and take a nap as soon as my brain is shutting down. Not to prolong the inevitable.

If I do not stop in a timely manner, when the tiredness starts it only makes the recovery longer. My tiredness is the sign to stop.

I need to take all my medication at the correct time. Especially the ones for heart palpitations. If taken late and palpitations fell so loud it seems like, I can feel them in my ears, I must lay down and do my relaxation therapy until they kick in. Calm down and nap.

I might be able to start turning the corner if I can get a proper routine back in my life if

possible. Get up shower, still wear relaxing clothes, but look and smell clean.

Then do things in bit size pieces. Prioritise things. Maybe even make lists like I would have done years ago to manage a project.

Make realistic targets for myself. Tomorrow is another day. What I did years ago is not

achievable today with my current condition. That said it is possible to achieve in bit side chunks. Ambition is not the key. Being aware of what my brain is capable of achieving is the key and balancing those precious moments. I need to keep my daily list short. Overly ambitious lists will only trigger the Dark days. I need to be fully aware of what triggers the Dark days and what does not.

Identify the things that exhaust me. Like playing the Wordscapes game on the iPad. Going shopping when there are too many people about.

Researching on the internet. Whether it be for my book or Jewellery findings and enjoyable as it is it exhausts me.

You know what they say too much of a good thing can be bad for you.

I had a really, true to life dream the other night. I was doing my old job of consulting in Royal Mail. Spending Monday to Friday away from home in Aberdeen. Then driving home just long enough to say hi to the cat and swap my washing and clothes for a trip to Birmingham to see Anne. For a girlie weekend. I was tired with all the driving, but Red Bull and black coffee always brought me round.

When I woke up my thoughts were seriously! Was I out of my mind? How the hell did I

keep going?

Well that was a warning. I cannot even drive at the moment. One of my favourite past times. My foot freezes up in pain on the accelerator. How many more pleasures do I need to lose before I learn that something has to change?

The Corona V has reached its peak. The country's tide will change now.

I need to change if I want to achieve things in the coming years. I need to change how I do things. All of us going forward need to revaluate what's safe to do and how best to manage the different world we need to live in.

I look forward to sharing my next adventure and stage two of the "The Dark Hat 2 -Survival of Madness" in my next book. I wish you all well with your new journeys in life.

Guess what I am going to do first. Sleep! Rest and More Sleep!

And back to the post its!

Dear Reader,

Apologies if anything I have written in this book is offensive to any of my readers. It is purely the ramblings of a mad woman who is trying to share how life has made her feel and in doing so enabling others to identify that they are not alone in Surviving madness.

Part 2 is being written as this goes to print and hopefully I will be able to share with you the next few months of mine and the countries recovery and look forward to seeing you at local book shops, craft fairs and mental health café's and clubs around the country where we can share experiences of how we have dealt with them.

If any of you would like me to hold a book signing on your premises please get in touch. I love to meet you and share life's experiences.

Remember being open and honest about what's going on in your brain is the only way you will truly start your journey to recovery.

I'll be trying to write other books about some of the crazy things I've done and adventures in life I've had so please look out for them on Facebook.

The Dark Hat two should be completed for Christmas.

Veronicaanjashaw@yahoo.com

Much Success and happiness to you all!

Veronica Anja Shaw

Veronica
Anja Shaw

Fifty years of suffering unknowingly from Anxiety and Depression, I've had to open pandora's painful box.

Endless Dark episodes of isolation and escaping from relationships and rejections. Dark moments hiding in Dark cupboards is finally too much for my brain to get over. Sitting , staring into oblivion detached from the world, it's time to address the trauma deep inside me.

No more denial. The Dark Hat life is not for me! I want to remove it for good! Will I succeed ? I really don't know. Come along with me on my honest journey of discovering what mental health really feels like.

Veronica A Shaw X